A CHURCH FOR RACHEL

MERCER
UNIVERSITY PRESS

Endowed by
TOM WATSON BROWN
and
THE WATSON-BROWN FOUNDATION, INC.

A Church for Rachel

SERMONS FOR THOSE WHO MOURN

Charles E. Poole

MERCER UNIVERSITY PRESS

MACON, GEORGIA

MUP/ H860

© 2012 Mercer University Press
1400 Coleman Avenue
Macon, Georgia 31207

First Edition

Books published by Mercer University Press are printed on acid-free
paper that meets the requirements of the American National
Standard for Information Sciences—Permanence of Paper for Printed
Library Materials.

Mercer University Press is a member of Green Press Initiative
(greenpressinitiative.org), a nonprofit organization working to help
publishers and printers increase their use of recycled paper and
decrease their use of fiber derived from endangered forests. This
book is printed on recycled paper.

Library of Congress Cataloging-in-Publication Data

Poole, Charles E.
  A church for Rachel : sermons for those who mourn / Charles E.
Poole.
    p. cm.
  ISBN-13: 978-0-88146-399-6 (alk. paper)
  ISBN-10: 0-88146-399-X (alk. paper)
  ISBN-13: 978-0-88146-377-4 (e-book)
  ISBN-10: 0-88146-377-9 (e-book)
  1. Consolation--Sermons. 2. Baptists--Sermons. I. Title.
  BV4905.3.P66 2012
  252'.56--dc23
                              2012022233

CONTENTS

PREFACE

There is a long list of ways things can go wrong in this life. None of us will experience all of them, but all of us will experience some of them. Most of them will be the expected sorrows of inevitable disease and natural death; some will be the more complex and lingering griefs of guilt and remorse; and a few will be sorrows so deep and severe that they tear our heart from our chest and leave us drowning in an ocean of agony, our spirits crushed by wave upon wave of fear, anger, disappointment, and pain.

These sermons seek to say a small word to those great sorrows. They are written for those who have found a seat on the mourners' bench; for those who are going through what cannot be gone around; for weary souls who are living through things that, had someone told them ahead of time they were going to have to go through, they would have sworn they would never make it.

But we do make it through. We do live into, through, and beyond the worst that life brings to us. We go through what cannot be gone around and, someday, we give up our seat on the mourners' bench to some other soul who once was happy but now is broken. We do get through, but not by our own power and not all by ourselves. In the face of our most crushing sorrow, "individualism" is exposed for the myth it is, and we learn how desperately we need the voices and faces of the people of God who embody the presence of God in our deepest darkness. As Stanley Hauerwas once wrote, "Courage is just another name for friends." Indeed, courage is another name for friends, and hope is, too. Hope is another name for friends and peace is another name for friends, and the strength to keep going is also another name for the people in our lives who are, to us, the face of God in the dark of pain.

When we find those caring friends in the family of faith, the family of faith becomes what I have come to call "a church for Rachel." In scripture, Old Testament and New, Jeremiah 31:15 and Matthew 2:18, Rachel weeps a river of tears. "Inconsolable" is the way she is described. Her sorrow is unconsolable because her losses are unrecoverable. So much is so over that too much is too over for Rachel.

When life becomes that difficult for us, when life becomes as bewildering, disappointing, and painful for us as it sometimes was for Rachel, we need "a church for Rachel"; a family of faith to sit beside us on the mourners' bench and walk beside us on the hard, hard way; a family of friends who won't let us go or drown or suffer alone. That's what we need, and, if we have a gentle, mindful, prayerful, compassionate family of faith, that's what we have: a church for the Rachels of this world, which, sooner or later, might be any of us, and will be many of us.

These sermons for those who mourn, these simple words for the weary Rachels of this world, were first offered to the deep, dear souls who worship God at Northminster, a true and tender "church for Rachel." The words that are gathered here found their way, across the years, from the wilderness of my handwriting to the order of typed legibility through the long-suffering diligence of Donna Lewis, Jan McDonnieal-Wilson, and Patsy Kerr, to whom I offer here my deep gratitude.

The dedication is to the Northminster family of faith, with more love and gratitude than words can tell or say.

Charles Eugene Poole
The Season of Pentecost
2011

A Church for Rachel

CAREFUL SPEECH

[1]Therefore, since we are justified by faith, we have peace with God through our Lord Jesus Christ, [2]through whom we have obtained access to this grace in which we stand; and we boast in our hope of sharing the glory of God. [3]And not only that, but we also boast in our sufferings, knowing that suffering produces endurance, [4]and endurance produces character, and character produces hope, [5]and hope does not disappoint us, because God's love has been poured into our hearts through the Holy Spirit that has been given to us.
—Romans 5:1–5

Those are very beautiful words Paul wrote to the Romans, all about how suffering makes us stronger and hope won't ever let us down, but every time I hear them I wonder how they sound to those whose suffering is most severe. How does "We rejoice in our suffering" sound in the ears of those who are truly suffering? During my years as a minister on the street I helped lead a worship service that met every Sunday afternoon in an abandoned apartment in west Jackson. The first time I went I sat next to a young man who has since died. Though he had been born healthy, he now could not see, speak, or walk. Across the years we became friends. I visited him in his home more times than I can count, but the only response he could make to my voice was an occasional groan or a violent wave of his arm in my direction. When I read, "We rejoice in our suffering," I think of him and wonder how those words would sound in his ears. Many years ago I had a friend who was a Holocaust survivor. His concentration camp number was still visible on his wrist. He told me once how, as a child, he had watched his mother's lifeless body be thrown from the box-car where he and she were traveling on one of Hitler's death trains. So I wonder what sort of sound "We rejoice in our suffering" might make in his ears. Or what about the woman whose story I read in a local newspaper in the summer of 2006? When she was four years old both her parents died, at which time she was taken in by a relative, at whose hands she suffered frequent and unspeakable abuse until she escaped at age twelve. I wonder what she thinks when she hears those wonderful old words, "We rejoice in our suffering."

I'm not saying we shouldn't say, "We rejoice in our suffering," but I am suggesting that when we say such glad and hopeful things, we should say them in a way that is mindful of the unresolved daily agony that millions of God's children suffer and bear. When we say, "We rejoice in our suffering," we should say it so carefully, and so mindfully of the enormity of human suffering, that our words will leave room in the room for those who are living in the deepest, darkest corners of pain and loss.

Once we have learned to say "We rejoice in our suffering" that carefully, mindfully, and quietly, then we are ready to say why we rejoice in our suffering: "We rejoice in our suffering because we know that suffering produces endurance, endurance produces character, and character produces hope." In other words, we rejoice in our suffering because good things sometimes grow in the soil of suffering. We rejoice in our suffering because suffering changes us in ways that comfort doesn't. I know that is true. I have lived a largely unscathed life, but even the small suffering I have known has never failed to soften my life toward others and open my life toward God. I, like many of you, can truly say, as the Psalmist said, "It is good for me that I have been afflicted."

So, Romans 5:3–4 rings true when it says that suffering produces good things. But even that we must say carefully, because while it is true, it is not automatic. Think of all the children of God for whom suffering did not produce endurance, children of God every bit as loved and redeemed as you and me who sought relief in death because they could not bear the unbearable one more day. "Suffering produces endurance" is a true and beautiful thing to say, but while it is true, it is not automatic, so even that must be spoken mindfully, thoughtfully, and carefully.

As must another truly beautiful phrase from Romans chapter 5, Paul's affirmation in verse 5 that "Hope does not disappoint us." Those are wonderful words for us to hear, but whenever I hear them, I think about all our faithful, hopeful sisters and brothers who have lived and died with dreams that had to be buried and hopes that never came true. When we read those wonderful words "Hope does not disappoint us," we have to be mindful of all the children of God who, despite a lifetime of hoping, are yet living with disappointments and sorrows they never imagined they would have to face. When we say, as Paul said, "Hope does not disappoint us," we must be careful to complete the sentence the way Paul completed it: "Hope does not disappoint us, because God's love has been poured into our hearts through the Holy Spirit." Paul doesn't say that hope does not disappoint us because our dreams come true or our lives go well or our problems get fixed. Instead, he says that our hope is never disappointed because our hearts are full of the love of God; God's love for us and our love for God. God loves us, no matter what, and we love God, no matter what. We believe God is good when our lives are wonderful and we believe God is good when our lives are awful. We've learned that life is what it is and God is who God is. That's why our hope is never disappointed, because it isn't the kind of hope that expects life to be good. Rather, it's the kind of hope that expects God to be good. Our hope is tied to nothing but the God we love, and since we love God the way God loves us, unconditionally, our hope is never disappointed. That's a great way to live, but not everybody is there yet, so even that we must say quietly and carefully, deeply mindful of the awful disappointment that some of God's children do feel, in God.

When it comes to the great mysteries of suffering and loss, pain and prayer, disappointment and hope, I invite you to a life of careful speech. We live in a Bible-belt world where the slogans and certitudes of popular Christianity are quick to squeeze orchestras of mystery so vast no stage can hold them into harmonicas of certainty so small any pocket can carry them, assigning everything, no matter how tragic or violent, to "God's plan." I invite you to embrace, instead, a more careful way of speaking about the mysteries of suffering and the ways of God, a way of speaking that is meticulously careful to obey that simple injunction in Romans 12:16, "Do not claim to be wiser than you are." In the face of the mystery of suffering, our task is to fall silent for a while and then, from that silence, to say wonderful old words in careful new ways. I invite you to learn to say "We rejoice in our suffering" in a careful, mindful, thoughtful voice that sounds as though it belongs more to someone who is struggling with hard questions than to someone who has settled for easy answers.

Amen.

INCURABLE HOPE

[13]The promise that he would inherit the world did not come to Abraham or to his descendants through the law but through the righteousness of faith. [14]If it is the adherents of the law who are to be the heirs, faith is null and the promise is void. [15]For the law brings wrath; but where there is no law, neither is there violation. [16]For this reason it depends on faith, in order that the promise may rest on grace and be guaranteed to all his descendants, not only to the adherents of the law but also to those who share the faith of Abraham (for he is the father of all of us, [17]as it is written, 'I have made you the father of many nations')—in the presence of the God in whom he believed, who gives life to the dead and calls into existence the things that do not exist. [18]Hoping against hope, he believed that he would become 'the father of many nations', according to what was said, 'So numerous shall your descendants be.' [19]He did not weaken in faith when he considered his own body, which was already as good as dead (for he was about a hundred years old), or when he considered the barrenness of Sarah's womb. [20]No distrust made him waver concerning the promise of God, but he grew strong in his faith as he gave glory to God, [21]being fully convinced that God was able to do what he had promised. [22]Therefore his faith 'was reckoned to him as righteousness.' [23]Now the words, 'it was reckoned to him,' were written not for his sake alone, [24]but for ours also. It will be reckoned to us who believe in him who raised Jesus our Lord from the dead, [25]who was handed over to death for our trespasses and was raised for our justification. —Romans 4:13–25

Every time I hear those words about Abraham's faith, I find myself thinking about William Sloane Coffin's wonderful old observation, "Faith has a limbering effect on the mind. By taking us beyond familiar ground, faith gives us so much more to think about."[1] Romans chapter 4 says that long after Abraham should've *given up*, something kept him *limbered up*. Something kept Abraham hoping on when every reason for hope was gone, and, according to Romans chapter 4, that something was faith. Though he was faced with a daunting set of troubling facts, Abraham never lost hope because Abraham's faith gave him something more to think about than just the facts on the ground.

As you will recall, the facts on the ground held no hope for Abraham. God had promised Abraham that his descendants would be more numerous than the stars in the sky, but, so far, no star. And, now, all reasonable prospects for a child are gone. That time is past. At least, so say the facts on the ground. But don't try to tell that to Abraham. It isn't that Abraham doesn't understand the facts, it's just that he has something else to think about in addition to the facts. Our lesson from Romans describes that something else with these words: "Hoping against hope, Abraham believed that he would become the father of many nations. When he faced the facts about his own body, which was already as good as dead, he did not weaken or waver, but grew strong in faith, being fully convinced that God was able to do what God had promised." Those words from Romans are Paul's theological reflection on Abraham and Sarah's story, the culmination of which is recorded in Genesis 21, which says, "Sarah conceived and bore Abraham a son when Abraham was a hundred years old. And Sarah said,

---

[1] William Sloane Coffin, *Credo* (Louisville: Westminster John Knox, 2005).

'God has made me laugh, and everyone who hears about this baby will laugh with me.'" Abraham lived an unyielding life of unwavering faith and, in the end, everybody laughed out loud because everything worked out fine.

So far so good, but now comes the hard part. The hard part is crossing the bridge from Abraham's story to ours without lapsing into that popular religious speech that says that if we, like Abraham, have enough faith, then we, like Abraham, will receive from God the healing or the child or the success or the protection or the blessing we most want, the converse assumption being that if we don't receive the blessing it is because we didn't have enough faith. That is what I call "transactional theology," the kind of theology that turns our life with God into a transaction in which God is the owner, we are the customers, and faith is the currency we must offer God enough of in order to obtain from God the outcome we desire. A lot of fine people believe that way, and I understand that the bookshelves and airways are heavily populated by that kind of thinking, but it doesn't ring true to me, because that way of thinking says that God has the power to step in and bring relief and healing and comfort to broken, hurting, devastated lives, but God will only step in and change things if we show God enough faith. God, in that way of thinking, is stuck in neutral, unable or unwilling to act in kindness and mercy unless and until we show enough faith. (There are Bible verses one can enlist in support of "transactional theology." For example, James 1:5–7 says that if we ask in faith we will receive, but only if we have enough faith. I know that there are those "transactional" verses in the Bible, but I believe we must start with what we believe about God and then interpret the Bible, not the other way around. No one loves the Bible more than I. The Bible is our deepest, dearest, most inspired and inspiring guide to God, but verses on pages do not fully define God. As Barbara Brown Taylor has wisely written, "To confuse the Bible with God is like confusing the field guide with the field."[2]) Since I don't believe our life with God is a series of transactions, I believe that faith, rather than being the currency we give to God, is the room we leave for God. To be a person of faith is to leave room in your life for the promise and possibility and joy and surprise of what God might yet do, no matter what the hopeless facts on the ground might say. That's how Abraham lived. Abraham left room in his life for the goodness of God. He lived open to the promise that God wasn't finished, through, over, or done, cold hard facts notwithstanding. It was that kind of leave-room-for-God faith that made Abraham a person of incurable hope.

Personally, I have never had as much faith as I would like to have, but I do have a pretty good case of incurable hope. I never fully recognized it until I spent four years serving as a minister on the street. Whenever people would ask me what I did and I would tell them about leading Bible classes in the parking lots of low-income apartment complexes in Jackson's most disadvantaged neighborhoods, the response would often be, "My goodness. Don't you get discouraged?" Sometimes I was tempted to say "Yes" so I would sound wise and reasonable. But, foolish as it may sound, there was never a moment when I doubted for a second that God would bring great good out of those tiny moments. I knew God was in on what I was up to, because I knew I was in on what God was up to. I had a severe case of incurable hope, and I can tell you, there's nothing like it. There's nothing like living a life of faith. It limbers up your soul and gives you so much more to think

---

[2] Barbara Brown Taylor, *Leaving Church* (San Francisco: Harper Collins, 2006) 216.

about than just the facts on the ground. Faith makes room in the room for God.

In the closing pages of *A Scandalous Providence*, Frank Tupper tells about an experience his wife had in the summer of 1983. A young wife and mother of two, Betty was nearing the end of a hard battle with an incurable disease when she said to Frank one evening, "I want to tell you something that happened to me this morning." Knowing her husband's rigorous mind, she added, "But I'm not sure you'll believe me." She went on to say that she had been praying for months for God to take away her fear of death, and that morning, while she was praying again that same prayer, she had felt herself embraced in an unusually strong sense of the presence of God. "Then," she said, "I heard children laughing. I heard children laughing on the Other Side." Frank Tupper said that, because he believes in the resurrection, he did believe what Betty told him. He then closed that story, and his book, by saying that, while Betty continued to be genuinely disappointed that her disease was not cured, she was never again afraid of the death through which she had to pass, because she had heard the laughter that lives over on the Other Side.[3]

That is what faith does. Even when faith does not defeat an incurable disease, it does create an incurable hope, because faith leaves room, even in deep darkness, for the promise and possibility and surprise and laughter and love of God. Faith never stops saying, "Who knows?" Who knows what God will yet do? Who knows what goodness and grace is waiting, on this side and on the Other Side? We don't know what's coming from God, but since, by faith, we believe that God is never

---

[3] Frank Tupper, *A Scandalous Providence* (Macon: Mercer University Press, 1995) 437.

finished, through, or done with anyone, we always know that something else is always coming. Something more is waiting. We cannot see it, but we do not doubt it, because we gladly suffer from a really bad case of incurable hope.

Amen.

TRUST

²² After these things God tested Abraham. He said to him, "Abraham!" And he said, "Here I am." ²He said, "Take your son, your only son Isaac, whom you love, and go to the land of Moriah, and offer him there as a burnt-offering on one of the mountains that I shall show you." ³So Abraham rose early in the morning, saddled his donkey, and took two of his young men with him, and his son Isaac; he cut the wood for the burnt-offering, and set out and went to the place in the distance that God had shown him. ⁴On the third day Abraham looked up and saw the place far away. ⁵Then Abraham said to his young men, "Stay here with the donkey; the boy and I will go over there; we will worship, and then we will come back to you." ⁶Abraham took the wood of the burnt-offering and laid it on his son Isaac, and he himself carried the fire and the knife. So the two of them walked on together. ⁷Isaac said to his father Abraham, "Father!" And he said, "Here I am, my son." He said, "The fire and the wood are here, but where is the lamb for a burnt-offering?" ⁸Abraham said, "God himself will provide the lamb for a burnt-offering, my son." So the two of them walked on together. ⁹When they came to the place that God had shown him, Abraham built an altar there and laid the wood in order. He bound his son Isaac, and laid him on the altar, on top of the wood. ¹⁰Then Abraham reached out his hand and took the knife to kill his son. ¹¹But the angel of the Lord called to him from heaven, and said, "Abraham, Abraham!" And he said, "Here I am." ¹²He said, "Do not lay your hand on the boy or do anything to him; for now I know that you fear God, since you have not withheld your son, your only son, from me." ¹³And Abraham looked up and saw a ram, caught in a thicket by its horns. Abraham went and took the

ram and offered it up as a burnt-offering instead of his son.
[14]So Abraham called that place "The Lord will provide"; as it is
said to this day, "On the mount of the Lord it shall be
provided." —Genesis 22:1–14

In Wendell Berry's novel *Jayber Crow*, there is a passage in
which Jayber is struggling to resolve his questions about God
and the Bible. He has just enrolled as a pre-ministerial student
at Pigeonville College, but "pre-ministerial" or not, he's having
some doubts. He goes to one of his religion professors and lays
out a litany of serious questions about God and the Bible, to
which the wise professor replies, "You have been given
questions to which you cannot be given answers."[1]

The same is true for us when we sit in the shadow of the
story of Abraham and Isaac on Mount Moriah. Every three
years the lectionary places this passage in our path, and every
three years it gives us questions to which we cannot be given
answers: Would the God we worship really use a person's
child to test a person's faith? Would the God who is revealed in
Jesus really create a situation where a child would be subjected
to the terror of thinking they were about to be killed? Is God
really like that, or is that only the way those who wrote the
Bible perceived God? Those are the kinds of questions that
deepen the shadows on Mt. Moriah, questions about both the
nature of God and the nature of the Bible. It is not a bad thing
to have such questions. Indeed, to have such questions is one
of the ways we keep the commandment to "love God with our
minds." (As William Sloane Coffin once observed, "Jesus came
to take away our sins, not our minds.")[2]

---

[1] Wendell Berry, *Jayber Crow* (Washington DC: Counterpoint, 2000)
54.

[2] This is a phrase I heard attributed to William Sloane Coffin.

In the face of such hard questions the temptation, of course, is to flood the honest darkness of Moriah's mystery with the synthetic light of easy answers. But that is a temptation to be resisted. We must be content to let the story's questions stand and to find, among the story's many questions, the story's central truth, which is that "God can be trusted." On the page and in the Bible, the story itself may be wrapped in a dozen layers of impenetrable, inscrutable mystery, but off the page and in our lives, the story's central truth is that, even when God cannot be explained or understood, God can be trusted.

God can be trusted is what Abraham said to Isaac at the most critical moment of the journey up the mountain. Abraham and Isaac were climbing Mt. Moriah, when young Isaac said to his dad, "I see the wood and I see the fire, but where is the lamb for the burnt offering?" We hold our breath. What will Abraham say? Will he tell Isaac what God has told him? Will he say "It's you, Isaac. The sacrifice is you." After all, that is what God told Abraham. "Well, yeah, but it's only a test." We know it's only a test, but Abraham doesn't. Abraham only knows what he has been told, and what he has been told is too awful for words; and, worst of all, he doesn't know the whole thing is just a test. But even in his awful darkness, he trusts that God will do something. So his answer to Isaac's question is simply, "The Lord will provide." The word "provide" in verse eight is translated from a Hebrew word that means "see to it." "What are we going to sacrifice, Dad?" "The Lord will see to that, Son. The Lord will see to it."

And God does see to it. God sees to it that the knife is caught in the air, the ram is caught in the bush, and Isaac comes home unharmed. And when all is said and done, the central point of the awful story is that God can be trusted. Or, as my good friend Helen Taliaferro says, "There's always a ram in the bush." One Thursday morning at Wood Street Bible Class, people were talking about life's worst sorrows and hardest losses. As Mrs. Taliaferro reflected on her own deepest griefs, she said with deep, quiet, battle-tested faith, "But through it all there's always been a ram in the bush." Or, as Abraham said, "The Lord will provide." Or as Easter tells us, God always has something else, something more, something new yet to do that we can't see and don't know.

Of course, such things as these we can only say quietly and carefully. When we say, "The Lord will provide," we must say it quietly and carefully, mindful of the fact that, while Abraham got his miracle, not everyone does. People do not get up on Sunday morning, get dressed, get in their cars, and go to church so they can be told cheerful-sounding things that will not stand up and prove true in life's toughest arenas. So let us be careful to say that not every story ends happily and not every situation gets fixed. Some people get the miracle they *want*, the kind of miracle that enables them to escape the worst sorrow. But others only get the miracle they *need*, the kind of miracle that enables them to endure the worst sorrow. Either way, God can be trusted—trusted to get us *around* the worst or to see us *through* the worst. God will provide...something. There will be some kind of ram in the bush, some gift from God. God will not abandon or forsake us. Even when God cannot be explained or understood or defended, even then God can be trusted.

Frederick Buechner tells a remarkable story about a time in his life when the Buechner family was going through a dreadful darkness. Buechner had pulled over to the side of a highway and was just sitting there on the roadside, immobilized by helplessness and fear. As he sat there, he looked up and saw an approaching car with one of those customized license plates. As the car drew near and drove past, Buechner read the letters on the front and back license plates: T R U S T.[3] He took it as a word from God. He later learned that the owner of the car worked in the trust department of a bank. But that didn't matter. He still took it as a word from God that came to him in the midst of his awful pain and deep fear.

I offer that word to you today. TRUST. I offer it to you as a word from God. TRUST. There will be times in our lives when God cannot be explained or understood, but there will never be a moment when God cannot be trusted.

Amen.

---

[3] Frederick Buechner, *A Room Called Remember* (San Francisco: Harper and Row, 1984) 150.

GOD IS GREAT, GOD IS GOOD

[21]Have you not known? Have you not heard? Has it not been told you from the beginning? Have you not understood from the foundations of the earth? [22]It is he who sits above the circle of the earth, and its inhabitants are like grasshoppers; who stretches out the heavens like a curtain, and spreads them like a tent to live in; [23]who brings princes to naught, and makes the rulers of the earth as nothing. [24]Scarcely are they planted, scarcely sown, scarcely has their stem taken root in the earth, when he blows upon them, and they wither, and the tempest carries them off like stubble. [25]To whom then will you compare me, or who is my equal? says the Holy One. [26]Lift up your eyes on high and see: Who created these? He who brings out their host and numbers them, calling them all by name; because he is great in strength, in power, not one is missing. [27]Why do you say, O Jacob, and speak, O Israel, "My way is hidden from the Lord, and my right is disregarded by my God"? [28] Have you not known? Have you not heard? The Lord is the everlasting God, the Creator of the ends of the earth. He does not faint or grow weary; his understanding is unsearchable. [29]He gives power to the faint, and strengthens the powerless. [30]Even youths will faint and be weary, and the young will fall exhausted; [31]but those who wait for the Lord shall renew their strength, they shall mount up with wings like eagles, they shall run and not be weary, they shall walk and not faint. —Isaiah 40:21–31

Few passages in all the Bible have given more new strength to more weary souls than those beautiful old words from Isaiah chapter 40: "Those who wait on the Lord will renew their strength, they shall mount up with wings like eagles, they shall run and not grow weary, they shall walk and not faint." Those words were probably first heard by the people of God sometime around 540 BC, after nearly fifty years of living in exile in Babylon. Their lives had taken a strange turn back there somewhere. Things had turned out in ways they never would have imagined. So much was so over that too much was too over for life to ever get back to normal. They must have been feeling a deep sense of disappointment or despair because this passage from Isaiah says that they had started saying things like "God has forgotten us" and "We have been disregarded by the Lord."

It was in response to that sense of separation from God, and those gnawing doubts about God, that Isaiah's words emerged; a swift river of strong words about the greatness and goodness of God. The passage begins by declaring the power and might and greatness of God: "Why do you say 'God has forgotten us' and 'We have been disregarded by the Lord'?" Have you not known? Have you not heard? Have you forgotten that I am the Lord who sits above the circle of the earth? The Lord is God, the creator of all that is. Lift up your eyes on high and see the stars. Because the Lord is mighty in power and great in strength, all of them are named, numbered and accounted for." All of which is to say, "God is great." To the weary, displaced children of God who've begun to wonder if God has left them or forgotten them or lost sight of them, Isaiah says, "Have you not known? Have you not heard? Have you forgotten? God is the creator of all that is; the star-flinging, galaxy-gleaming, moon-rolling, ocean-bowling, sun-shining, lightning-striking, cloud-puffing, fish-finning, zebra-striping, giraffe-necking, whale-blowing, surf-foaming, day-breaking king of the universe." God, Isaiah reminded them, is still up there, still out there, still as mighty and powerful and great as ever. God is great.

And not only that, says Isaiah, not only is God great, God is also good. After all, God could be great, as in powerful and mighty, but if God didn't care about God's people, then God's greatness would be small comfort to weary souls in need of hope and strength. But Isaiah says God is not only great up in the sky, God is also good down on the ground: "Have you not known?" he asks. "Have you not heard? God gives strength to the weary and power to the powerless.... Those who wait on the Lord shall renew their strength. They shall mount up with wings like eagles, they shall run and not grow weary, they shall walk and not faint." With those words, Isaiah declared the goodness of God. God isn't just great up in the sky where the stars are, God is also good down on the ground where the scars are. God doesn't just look down on us from a lofty perch of power, God comes down to us on the weary way of struggle. God is great up in the sky we can see far, and God is good down on the ground where we are.

God is great. God is good. That was Isaiah's answer for weary souls then and now. It is a powerful, beautiful, hope-filled, life-lifting reminder that the God who is with us and for us is mighty, powerful, big, and great, and the God who is mighty, powerful, big, and great is with us and for us. God is great and God is good. Knowing, hearing, trusting, and believing that God is both great and good can make us glad and give us peace; but it can also make us wonder: If God is both great and good, great as in powerful and good as in kind, great in the sky and good on the ground, then how and why do so many terrible, awful, unbearable things manage to happen in this world? If God is both great *and* good, all powerful *and* all loving, how did that gunman ever get into the Amish schoolhouse in Pennsylvania back in October of 2006 and murder those five children? If God is both great and good, one would think that perhaps God might swoop down, step in, and stop such things. And sometimes God does, praise God. But sometimes God doesn't, which isn't easy to understand given the fact that God is both great, as in powerful, and good, as in kind. "Well, yeah, but God doesn't send those awful things, God just allows them." I used to say that, but then one day it occurred to me that to say that God had the power to stop something evil and horrible but allowed it to happen anyway is to assign to God a level of permissiveness that we would find intolerable in one another, so I don't say that anymore. "Well, yeah, but God has purposes that are accomplished as a result of awful tragedies." I think I probably used to say that, too. But then one day it occurred to me that if God can endlessly fling out stars, easily throw down lightning, and daily doll up dusk, then God can probably also accomplish God's purposes without destroying innocent lives, so I don't say that anymore, either.

There is great mystery here—irresolvable, unknowable, unsayable mystery. I would prefer not to mention the mystery, but I raise it because every wonderful, hopeful word we say about the greatness and goodness of God must be a word that rings true in the ears of whomever in the world is most heartsick, disappointed, and broken by life. The things we say in church about God and life must withstand the scrutiny of the world's most tearful eyes. To say, "God is great and God is good" is both to shine a light of peace and to cast a shadow of mystery. Claiming the light without naming the shadow may be sufficient for those who have only known life's usual sorrows and natural griefs, but it leaves something unsaid for those whose world has been torn asunder by inexplicable tragedy and unbearable pain. Careful speech about God requires us to embrace the light that shines from, and the shadows that fall around, the simple, central truth that God is great and God is good. For the worst of those shadows, we have no satisfactory answer. In the end, we are left at last to trust and love where we cannot understand or explain.

At the end of life's long line of unanswered questions there is only faith's deep well of unconditional love—not just God's for us, but also ours for God. There is nothing in all the world quite so liberating as loving God without the answers, loving God through the shadows, loving God unconditionally with never a thought about being protected, blessed, or spared in return. That's the way we love the Lord—the same way the Lord loves us, unconditionally, no strings attached. We love the Lord, trust the Lord, and, as Isaiah said, "We wait on the Lord for the strength to walk and not faint." We trust the Lord to see us through what the Lord did not spare us from. And, sure enough, we receive from the Lord the strength to keep moving, to get through, to walk and not faint. And if we do faint, if we become so weary or sad or depleted that we faint and fall down, the Lord we've been waiting on will wait on us. The great, good God we love and trust will curl up next to us and lie down beside us until we're ready to get up and go again. That's how good the great God is. God is great, way up there where the rain and the stars are, and God is good, way down here where the pain and the scars are.

Amen.

Unanswered, Unsettled, Unsolved

[1]My God, my God, why have you forsaken me? Why are you so far from helping me, from the words of my groaning? [2]O my God, I cry by day, but you do not answer; and by night, but find no rest. [3]Yet you are holy, enthroned on the praises of Israel. [4]In you our ancestors trusted; they trusted, and you delivered them. [5]To you they cried, and were saved; in you they trusted, and were not put to shame. [6]But I am a worm, and not human; scorned by others, and despised by the people. [7]All who see me mock at me; they make mouths at me, they shake their heads; [8]"Commit your cause to the Lord; let him deliver—let him rescue the one in whom he delights!" [9]Yet it was you who took me from the womb; you kept me safe on my mother's breast. [10]On you I was cast from my birth, and since my mother bore me you have been my God. [11]Do not be far from me, for trouble is near and there is no one to help. [12]Many bulls encircle me, strong bulls of Bashan surround me; [13]they open wide their mouths at me, like a ravening and roaring lion. [14]I am poured out like water, and all my bones are out of joint; my heart is like wax; it is melted within my breast; [15]my mouth is dried up like a potsherd, and my tongue sticks to my jaws; lay me in the dust of death. —Psalm 22:1–15

[1]Then Job answered: [2]"Today also my complaint is bitter; his hand is heavy despite my groaning. [3]O that I knew where I might find him, that I might come even to his dwelling! [4]I would lay my case before him, and fill my mouth with arguments. [5]I would learn what he would answer me, understand what he would say to me. [6] Would he contend with me in the greatness of his power? No; but he would give heed to me. [7]There an upright person could reason with him,

and I should be acquitted for ever by my judge. ⁸If I go forward, he is not there; or backward, I cannot perceive him; ⁹on the left he hides, and I cannot behold him; I turn to the right, but I cannot see him. ¹⁶ God has made my heart faint; the Almighty has terrified me; ¹⁷ If only I could vanish in darkness, thick darkness would cover my face!" Job 23:1–9, 16–17

Based on that pair of scripture lessons, I don't think anyone will be nominating our old friend Lex for "Mr. Sunshine" anytime soon. I'm talking about our Sunday morning Bible passage-picking friend, Lex Shunnairy. What was the lectionary thinking when it assigned Psalm 22 *and* Job 23 to be read on the same Sunday? Wouldn't either of those passages, all by itself, have been sufficiently serious for a single Sunday? After all, Job 23 can't find God and Psalm 22 can't reach God. Job 23 wonders where God has gone and Psalm 22 wonders why God has gone. Either of them, all alone, could sing a sad solo, *but both of them? On the same Sunday?* That's just agony in harmony: "My God, my God, why have you forsaken me? Why are you so far from helping me?" sings the Psalm, and Job chimes in with, "My complaint is bitter, because I cannot find God." "Where is God?" Job thunders. "Why isn't God helping us?" the Psalm wonders. *Where? Why?…Where? Why?*

But, ironically enough, despite the bitterness of their complaints and the fierceness of their questions, we're actually sort of glad to have them both in the same church on the same day. As it turns out, it's actually sort of comforting to us when Psalm 22 and Job 23 come as a couple, asking "Where?" and "Why?" about God and life, because that way we get to wrap their Bible verse voices around our own deepest questions about God and suffering, prayer and pain: "Why didn't God protect her or heal him or spare them? If God answered that prayer why not this prayer? If God ever heals anyone why not always everyone? Why does God, who in some cases seems to do so much, in other cases seem to do so little?" Those of us who are people of faith occasionally have moments when we ask those kinds of questions; moments when we know exactly what Psalm 22 and Job 23 are talking about; moments in our lives when we know the deep truth of Peter DeVries' unforgettable lament, "*Why*? is the question mark that is twisted like a fish hook in the heart."[1]

I cannot speak for you, but in my own life with God I have found that it is far better to *ask* "Why?" than it is to *say* why. There once was a time when I thought that, in the face of sudden tragedy or endless struggle, people of faith should always be able to say why, to offer an answer or an explanation, usually something along the lines of "God has a reason for this" or "God makes no mistakes" or "God had to send this to accomplish some other purpose," all intended to defend the sovereignty of God by placing the tragedy in the will of God and the plan of God. While I no longer use such phrases myself, I can certainly understand why so many people find so much comfort in phrases such as those. After all, they do at least make a little sense out of the inexplicable losses that break our hearts and change our lives while simultaneously defending God's level of involvement in, and control over, the world. So, of course, it is understandable that many people, in the face of tragedy and suffering, reach for words that assign all this pain and loss to some larger plan of God's. And, anyway, everyone must be free to assign their own meaning to their own pain. In her book *An Altar in the World*, Barbara Brown Taylor writes, "The meaning we give to

---

[1] Peter De Vries, *The Blood of the Lamb* (Boston: Little, Brown and Company, 1969) 243.

what happens in our lives is our final freedom."[2] She's right. We all get to assign our own meaning to our own sorrow, which for many people means saying that every awful thing that happens is in God's will and part of God's plan. But for me those explanations, those efforts to say why, just don't ring true. Take, for example, the tragic deaths of the young. I don't believe the tragic deaths of the young are in God's will or part of God's plan. Rather, I believe, with William Sloane Coffin, that when the young die tragically, "God's heart is, of all hearts, most broken."[3] Or take, for example, the horrific and endless abuse of a child, day after day, night after night, year upon brutal year. I don't believe that is in God's will or part of God's plan. Do you? I know we try to give God a loophole by saying that "God did not send it, God only allowed it," but that would mean God saw it, knew about it, had the power to stop it, and decided instead to let it continue, to *allow* it, in which case saying "God didn't send it, God just allowed it" ends up indicting the God we intended to defend.

Well, you see why I say it is far better to *ask* "Why?" than it is to *say* why. In his book *Lament for a Son*, Nicholas Wolterstorff gives us a beautiful example of a heartbroken soul content to *ask* "Why?" without then rushing forward to *say* why. Concerning the tragic death of his young son, Wolterstorff writes, "I cannot make it all fit together by saying, 'God did it,' but neither can I make it all fit together by saying, 'There was nothing God could do about it.' I do not know why God did not prevent Eric's death.... To the most agonizing

---

[2] Barbara Brown Taylor, *An Altar in the World* (New York: Harper Collins, 2009) 182.

[3] *A Chorus of Witnesses*, ed. Thomas G. Long and Cornelius Plating (Grand Rapids: Eerdman[s], 1994) 264.

question I have ever asked, I do not know the answer."[4] That may be faith's final frontier; to be content to *ask* "Why?" without then trying to *say* why. That is the kind of patient, tender, waiting faith Rainer Maria Rilke called us to embrace when he wrote, "Be patient toward all that remains unsolved in your heart."[5] That may very well be faith's final frontier; to love unconditionally the God we cannot understand, to pray constantly to the God we cannot control, to trust completely the God we cannot explain, and to live patiently with all that remains unanswered, unsettled and unsolved in our hearts.

Or, as one wise soul once said, *"Faith is what you have left when you don't get the miracle."*[6]

Amen.

---

[4] Nicholas Wolterstorff, *Lament for a Son* (Grand Rapids: Eerdmans, 1987) 67.

[5] Rainer Maria Rilke, *Letters to a Young Poet* (Novato: New World Library, 2000).

[6] I heard this saying attributed to Barbara Brown Taylor, but I cannot find it in print.

DANCING WITH THE SCARS

⁴⁶Mary said, "My soul magnifies the Lord, ⁴⁷my spirit rejoices in God my savior, ⁴⁸for he has looked with favour on the lowliness of his servant. Surely, from now on all generations will call me blessed; ⁴⁹for the Mighty One has done great things for me, and holy is his name. ⁵⁰His mercy is for those who fear him from generation to generation. ⁵¹He has shown strength with his arm; he has scattered the proud in the thoughts of their hearts. ⁵²He has brought down the powerful from their thrones, and lifted up the lowly; ⁵³he has filled the hungry with good things, and sent the rich away empty. ⁵⁴He has helped his servant Israel, in remembrance of his mercy, ⁵⁵according to the promise he made to our ancestors, to Abraham and to his descendants for ever." —Luke 1:46–55

To hear her sing, you'd think Mary hadn't a care in the world. One imagines that Mary must have had a head full of questions and a heart full of cares. After all, she had recently learned she was expecting a baby she wasn't expecting; and not just any baby, but the Savior of the world. So...*How would this change her life? Would anyone believe her story? What did all this mean?* If Mary was a real human being with hopes and fears and plans and dreams, then Mary must have had a head full of questions and a heart full of cares. And yet, in the face of all she had to think about, Mary managed to sing that joyful song, "My soul praises the Lord, and my spirit rejoices in God my Savior." Mary's mind may have been full of questions, but still she had room in her heart for joy. Mary's life wasn't simple or settled, safe or secure, and yet, she sang, "My soul praises the Lord, and my spirit rejoices in God my Savior."

Mary made room for joy in a life that was turning out in ways she never would have planned, and if we are going to have joy, we will have to do the same. The question, of course, is "How?" How do we make room for joy in lives where so much of the space has already been claimed by loss or grief, disappointment or anger, fear or shame, regret or fatigue? There are no quick and easy answers to those kinds of questions, but if you watch carefully the lives of those who have learned to live joyfully despite the fact that their lives have turned out in ways they never would have planned, one of the virtues they all seem to share is a quiet sense of contentment. We must be careful, of course, when we talk about contentment. After all, there are plenty of circumstances with which no one should be content. There are wrongs to be righted and injustices to be confronted. There are situations that cannot be endured and evils that must not be tolerated, not to mention habits to be conquered, addictions to be battled, callings to be followed, remedies to be sought, and cycles to be broken. I am not advocating the kind of contentment that lapses into complacency, but rather the kind of contentment that comes to terms with the things that cannot be changed, the kind of contentment that looks at life as it is and says, "I may wish I had a different life, but I don't. I may wish life had given me a different kind of mind or body or skills or talents, but it didn't. My life is what it is. It isn't perfect, but even if I had the life of my dreams, that life wouldn't be perfect either because the truth is, even at its best, life only gets so good." That's the kind of contentment of which I am speaking, the kind of contentment that is always at the bottom and center of joy.

Not long ago I ran across a phrase that captures that kind of contentment in a powerful and beautiful way. It was in a collection of spiritual memoirs called *Pilgrim Souls*. In a chapter on Emily Dickinson, the editors wrote that Dickinson had learned to be content with the narrow boundaries of her limited life in small-town New England because "Her soul had reached a settlement with her life."[1] To say that your soul has reached a settlement with your life is a much more poetic way of saying that you have come to terms with your reality; you have accepted the things that cannot be changed, which is the first and most fundamental step toward making room for joy in our less-than-perfect lives. Our only other option is to sacrifice joy and gladness on the altar of "if only": "If only that hadn't happened to us.... If only we didn't have to live with this.... If only I hadn't done that." The opposite of "if only," of course, is "even though": "Even though my life has turned out in ways I never would have dreamed, planned, or imagined, I will make room for joy. This is my life, and even though it doesn't exactly tally with the life of my fondest dreams, it will have to be the scene of my greatest joys.... I have no other life to turn to, after all, so even though this one isn't perfect, I will stay open to joys large and small. I will embrace them and pay attention to them and love them as they come, because to do otherwise would be to sacrifice the joy I can have on the altar of the joy I can't have."

I saw some of that *even though* joy one beautiful autumn evening a few years ago. Marcia and I did something that day we almost never do; we got all dressed up and went dancing. (Well, actually, we went to a wedding reception where they had some dancing.) As the evening wore on and the band played on, the dance floor became more and more crowded. At some point, I looked around at all those people, and it occurred to me that I knew almost every one of them. Because I knew

---

[1] Amy Mandelker and Elizabeth Powers, *Pilgrim Souls* (New York: Simon and Schuster, 1999) 65.

most of them pretty well, I knew that none of them had waltzed their way through life. Most of them had been through some deep valley or were facing some dark shadow. They'd all known their share of loss or sorrow, disappointment or pain. But, to see them dance, you'd think they hadn't a care in the world. None of them would have advanced to the finals on *Dancing with the Stars*, but all of them were doing a magnificent job of dancing with the *scars*. Apparently, their souls had reached some sort of settlement with their lives, enabling them to dance the way Mary sang; with great joy, *even though*.

Given the fact that none of our lives are perfect, that may be the only way any of us will ever dance or sing: dancing with the scars and singing for joy, *even though*....

Amen.

HELPLESS

²²And when the time came for their purification according to the law of Moses, they brought him up to Jerusalem to present him to the Lord ²³(as it is written in the law of the Lord, "Every firstborn male shall be designated as holy to the Lord"), ²⁴and they offered a sacrifice according to what is stated in the law of the Lord, "a pair of turtle-doves or two young pigeons." 25There was a man in Jerusalem whose name was Simeon; this man was righteous and devout, looking forward to the consolation of Israel, and the Holy Spirit rested on him. ²⁶It had been revealed to him by the Holy Spirit that he would not see death before he had seen the Lord's Messiah. ²⁷Guided by the Spirit, Simeon came into the temple; and when the parents brought in the child Jesus, to do for him what was customary under the law, ²⁸Simeon took him in his arms and praised God, saying, ²⁹"Master, now you are dismissing your servant in peace, according to your word; ³⁰for my eyes have seen your salvation, ³¹which you have prepared in the presence of all peoples, ³²a light for revelation to the Gentiles and for glory to your people Israel." ³³The child's father and mother were amazed at what was being said about him. ³⁴Then Simeon blessed them and said to his mother Mary, "This child is destined for the falling and the rising of many in Israel, and to be a sign that will be opposed ³⁵so that the inner thoughts of many will be revealed—and a sword will pierce your own soul too." ³⁶There was also a prophet, Anna the daughter of Phanuel, of the tribe of Asher. She was of a great age, having lived with her husband for seven years after her marriage, ³⁷then as a widow to the age of eighty-four. She never left the temple but worshipped there with fasting and prayer night and day. ³⁸At that moment she came, and began to praise God

and to speak about the child to all who were looking for the redemption of Jerusalem. [39]When they had finished everything required by the law of the Lord, they returned to Galilee, to their own town of Nazareth. [40]The child grew and became strong, filled with wisdom; and the favour of God was upon him. —Luke 2:22–40

One imagines that Simeon did not get invited to a lot of baby dedications, not after what happened in Luke chapter 2. He started out fine, talking about how wonderful baby Jesus was and how he would grow up to do great things, but then he went and threw a shadow over the whole day when he concluded his dedicatory litany with that ominous warning to Mary, "*And a sword will pierce your own soul, too.*" Mary must have wondered why Simeon would say such a thing. How could being the mother of this special child ever send a sword through her soul?

Of course, as the years went by, Mary would come to know exactly what Simeon meant when he said that someday she would feel a sword pierce her soul. For one thing, there was the conflict between Jesus and his brothers. According to John chapter 7, Jesus made claims about his relationship with God that his brothers simply did not believe. That conflict between her adult children was one Mary was helpless to fix, and it must have seemed at times like a sword in her soul. Then there's that passage in Matthew chapter 12, where someone comes to Jesus while he is teaching and says, "*Your mother and your brothers are outside. They want to talk to you.*" We would expect a good son to say, "*Sure. You all hold that thought while I take this call from my mom.*" But, instead, Jesus said, "*Who are my mother and my brothers? My disciples are my mother and my brothers.*" That had to feel at least a little like a sword through the soul of the mother who was left at the door, waiting in the hall to speak to her own son. And then, of course, there came the cross. According to the gospel accounts, Mary was there, present and helpless at the suffering of her son. So, needless to say, when that sword sliced his side, it pierced her own soul, too.

Without doubt, Mary and Jesus are a special case. They are in so many ways so very different from you and me, except for what Simeon said about the sword in the soul. What Simeon called "the sword in the soul" was something many have in common with Mary the mother of our Lord, something that might best be called *"helpless love."* As different as Mary and Jesus may be from you and me, our lives do intersect theirs at the corner where helplessness meets love. Once Jesus became an adult, Mary was helpless to manage his life, control his actions, or guard his safety, which meant that sometimes she felt that sword in the soul that Simeon said she would, because, while she was helpless to manage Jesus' decisions and guard Jesus' safety, she was also helpless to distance herself from Jesus' pain and suffering. That is the way full-grown love always ends—in helplessness. When we grew up to adulthood, we made those who love us helpless, and those we love will eventually make us helpless, too. Love between adults cannot be anything but helpless. We are helpless to manage the lives of those we love and we are also helpless to distance ourselves from the pain of those we love; helpless to control and protect, we are also helpless to love less.

If all this sounds a bit painful, it is. But this is the inevitable pain of that healthy love that lets go of control and management, and simply loves. This is love's last stand and final frontier, helpless love, love at its deepest, strongest, and purest. In fact, ponder this: Ponder the possibility that when we love someone we cannot manage or save but whose pain we cannot keep from bearing, that may be when our love is actually most like God's. What if it turned out that when we are loving most helplessly we are most like God? We don't often use both those words in the same sentence, "*helpless*" and "*God*," but the truth is, we have already seen God make God's own self helpless to do anything but watch and love and hurt with God's own grown child. When Jesus cried out from the cross, "*My God, my God, why have you forsaken me?*" God made God's own self helpless to step in and rescue God's own child from all that pain and humiliation and death. Sometimes people say that when Jesus cried out from the cross, "*My God, my God, why have you forsaken me?*" it was because God had turned away from Jesus because Jesus was bearing the sin of the world and God was too holy to watch. That is a popular saying, but I don't believe it. To the contrary, I believe the exact opposite. I believe that God was never more fully present with Jesus than at the death of Jesus—watching, hurting, aching, and loving, but loving in a way that left God helpless to rescue, spare, protect, or save Jesus.

Perhaps, even for God, love's last stand and final frontier is helplessness. Perhaps when you and I are left at last to love those we cannot manage, control, or protect, perhaps when we are left at last to love helplessly, we are then most like God. I always thought it was when we were most powerful and in control of things that we were most like God. But what if it turned out that we are most like God when we are helplessly loving...loving helplessly?

A Catholic priest named Father Gallenger once said, "Our choice in life is not a choice between pain and no pain, but only a choice between the pain of loving and the pain of not loving."[1] It's true. The deeper the love, the greater the pain. But

---

[1] This quote is borrowed from a sermon by John Claypool.

there is no other option, except not to love, and not to love would be not to live. So on we go; loving helplessly... helplessly loving.

    Amen.

WE CAN'T *NOT* PRAY

[11]He was praying in a certain place, and after he had finished, one of his disciples said to him, "Lord, teach us to pray, as John taught his disciples." [2]He said to them, "When you pray, say: Father, hallowed be your name. Your kingdom come. [3]Give us each day our daily bread. [4]Forgive us our sins, for we ourselves forgive everyone indebted to us. And do not bring us to the time of trial." [5]Then he said to them, "Suppose one of you has a friend, and you go to him at mid night and say to him, 'Friend, lend me three loaves of bread; [6]for a friend of mine has arrived, and I have nothing to set before him.' [7]And he answers from within, 'Do not bother me; the door has already been locked, and my children are with me in bed; I cannot get up and give you anything.' [8]I tell you, even though he will not get up and give him anything because he is his friend, at least because of his persistence he will get up and give him whatever he needs. [9]So I say to you, Ask, and it will be given to you; search, and you will find; knock, and the door will be opened for you. [10]For everyone who asks receives, and everyone who searches finds, and for everyone who knocks, the door will be opened. [11]Is there anyone among you who, if your child asks for a fish, will give a snake instead of a fish? [12]Or if the child asks for an egg, will give a scorpion? [13]If you then, who are evil, know how to give good gifts to your children, how much more will the heavenly Father give the Holy Spirit to those who ask him!" —Luke 11:1–13

There is nothing I do more of, and know less about, than prayer. Like many others, I spend much of my day praying. I start the day, almost every day, by writing in a prayer journal. Then, all through the day, much of what I do is pray. I pray while I'm driving, I pray while I'm walking across parking lots and through hospitals, and, before almost every meeting or appointment or planned conversation, I pray to be a person of careful speech. I don't mean to suggest that mine is a life of constant prayer, but it is a life of frequent prayer. So, when it comes to prayer, there's not much I do more of.

And there's not much I know less about. Prayer is our simplest gift and our greatest mystery. The mystery, of course, has to do with the fact that we don't know what prayer does to God. We know exactly what prayer does to us. Prayer centers us and strengthens us. Prayer gives us peace and courage and wisdom and insight. The life of prayer makes us quieter and kinder, less arrogant and judgmental, more truthful, innocent, agendaless, and pure. About that, there is no mystery. If you practice a disciplined, daily life of prayer, you know all that.

The mystery is not, "What does prayer do to us?" The mystery is, "What does prayer do to God?" The most popular answer to that question is, "Prayer causes God to give us what we pray for," which is understandable, given the presence in scripture of words such as those we find in Luke 11:9 and 10, "Ask and it will be given you.... For everyone who asks receives." Add to that John 14:14, "If in my name you ask me for anything I will do it"; John 15:16, "The Father will give you whatever you ask in my name"; John 16:23, "If you ask anything of the Father in my name he will give it to you"; and James 4:2, "You have not because you ask not," and it's little wonder that we assume that prayer is the way we get God to give us what we need. That is, after all, what those verses seem to say. The problem, of course, is that those verses and our lives don't always tally very well with each other. If you've done much praying, you know that sometimes what you ask happens and sometimes it doesn't, an undeniable fact of life that leads to all sorts of explanations that are offered in an effort to solve the mystery of why sometimes, when we ask, we do receive, and sometimes, when we ask, we don't receive. You've heard those explanations. They tend to sound like loopholes for God, and they usually go something like this: *"If you had prayed with more faith, God would have answered." "If you had prayed harder or longer, God would have known you were serious." "If you had gotten more people to join you in praying, God would not have been able to resist all those prayers."*

Think about what all those explanations about prayer say about God. They say that God has to be persuaded to do for us good things that God already knows we need, but that God will not do unless we give God enough faith or persistence or voices. That turns prayer into a transaction, in which we have to give God a certain amount of faith or level of persistence or number of prayer partners before God can be persuaded to help us. God is better than that. As Jesus said in Luke 11, God is better than a sleepy friend who has to be badgered into helping us. God doesn't have to be badgered, convinced, or impressed by our faith or perseverance or persistence in order to be persuaded to help us.

All of this leaves us with our unresolved, irresolvable mystery: *If God sometimes gives us the good thing for which we pray, why not every time?* I'm not talking about the trinkets and gadgets and luxuries and victories and bonuses for which we pray. I'm talking about our earnest, ardent prayers for deliverance and healing and clear biopsies and healthy babies and safe children. If God sometimes answers those prayers, why not always? I will never forget sitting one day in the intensive care waiting room at the Blair E. Batson Children's Hospital with a minister whose daughter was soon to die. As he reflected on the tragic church bus accident that ended her life, he said, *"When it was time for the kids to board the bus in the church parking lot, I was the one who led the prayer for their safe travel."* If God sometimes answers that kind of prayer, why not always? One of the most honest efforts I've ever heard anyone make at facing all that mystery came from theologian Frank Tupper. In response to a question about why some people get the answer for which they pray, while others who pray with equal faith and intensity don't, Frank replied, *"I don't know. I guess that, in every situation, God does all that God can do."*[1]

What else can we say? Prayer is our most simple gift and our most inscrutable mystery. It isn't magic and it isn't a transaction and it isn't the way we control life and manage God by getting God to do our will. At the end of the day, when all is said and done, prayer is the deepest, dearest way we have of trusting God and loving each other. When we pray, we tell God what we want and need and hope, and then we trust God to help us. We trust God to do what is best. We trust God to do all that God can do. Prayer is the way we trust God. And prayer is the way we love each other. To pray for someone is a deep, dear act of love and care—a strong, tender act of love and care that matters and makes a difference, sometimes in ways we get to see and celebrate, and sometimes in ways we will never know.

Basically, what it all comes down to is this: Prayer is the deepest, dearest, highest, strongest, truest way we have of trusting God and loving one another. So, of course, we pray all through the day. Of course we pray without ceasing. We couldn't keep ourselves from praying if we tried. *We can't not pray.*

Amen.

---

[1] This quote is borrowed from a sermon by Frank Tupper.

WHATEVER WE ASK?

⁹As the Father has loved me, so I have loved you; abide in my love. ¹⁰If you keep my commandments, you will abide in my love, just as I have kept my Father's commandments and abide in his love. ¹¹I have said these things to you so that my joy may be in you, and that your joy may be complete. ¹²This is my commandment, that you love one another as I have loved you. ¹³No one has greater love than this, to lay down one's life for one's friends. ¹⁴You are my friends if you do what I command you. ¹⁵I do not call you servants any longer, because the servant does not know what the master is doing; but I have called you friends, because I have made known to you everything that I have heard from my Father. ¹⁶You did not choose me but I chose you. And I appointed you to go and bear fruit, fruit that will last, so that the Father will give you whatever you ask him in my name. ¹⁷I am giving you these commands so that you may love one another. —John 15:9–17

I don't know about you, but I have often found myself wishing that prayer would always be as simple on the ground as it sometimes sounds on the page. Take, for example, John chapter 15, where Jesus says, *"I appointed you to go and bear fruit, so that the Father will give you whatever you ask him in my name."* On the page, that sounds simple, certain, and sure enough. In fact, the *"whatever you ask"* part actually sounds a little like a guarantee. And, in that regard, it is not alone. For example, John 15:7 says, *"If you abide in me, and my words abide in you, ask for whatever you wish and it will be done for you."* Then there is John 16:23, where Jesus says, *"Very truly I tell you, if you ask anything of the Father in my name, he will give it to you,"* not to mention Matthew 18:19, where Jesus declares, *"Truly I tell you, if two of you agree on earth about anything you ask, it will be done for you by my Father in heaven."* If you've ever done much praying, you already know that sometimes things do work out exactly that way. Sometimes we do receive *whatever we ask.* We get the relief or the healing or the answer or the blessing for which we so ardently prayed. Thanks be to God, it happens that way. Sometimes. Other times we pray just as long and just as hard with just as much faith and we do not receive *whatever we ask.* Now, we've all been around the church block enough times to know that this is the point in the sermon where the preacher is supposed to say something about how God sometimes says *Yes* and sometimes *No* and sometimes *Wait,* but that is not what those *whatever we ask* verses say. What the *whatever we ask* verses say is that we will receive *whatever we ask.* Careful speech requires us to say that sometimes it happens exactly the way that sounds and sometimes it doesn't.

Often, when I think about all this, I travel back to a hot summer day in July 2007. A good friend who was battling a serious disease had asked me to meet him for lunch so that we could talk about death and dying. (Which, for him, was rapidly approaching.) Somewhere in the course of the conversation, my friend said, *"When the Bible says that if we ask for anything in Jesus' name we will receive it, anything must not mean everything, because, if anything meant everything, I'd be well by now, because lots of people have been asking, in Jesus' name, for me to be healed. So,"* he concluded, *"anything must not mean everything, but it does mean something."* My friend was right. When the Bible says we will receive anything we ask in Jesus' name, *anything* apparently does not mean *everything,* but it certainly does mean *something*—something big and beautiful, hope-filled, and glad, but something that also sometimes leaves us with unsolvable mystery and irresolvable questions.

I don't have the answers to those questions, but after a lifetime of asking, seeking, and knocking, this much I can say with absolute certainty: *Sometimes prayer changes our lives and sometimes life changes our prayers.* Sometimes prayer changes our lives. I've seen it happen, and so have you. I'm talking about those times when we pray for the relief or the healing or the resolution or the deliverance and it comes; those glad and glorious times when, in the words of John 15:16, we receive *"Whatever we ask."* Sometimes it happens that way. Those are the times when prayer changes our lives. Then there are those other times when life changes our prayers. I'm talking about those times when our prayers keep moving in an effort to catch up to our lives; those times when we pray for what we want and don't receive it, so then we pray for the next-best thing and then the next-best thing after that until finally the only thing left to pray for is the strength and courage to go through that which we had previously prayed to go around. It happens that way sometimes. Sometimes, our prayers just have to keep moving in the direction where our life is going. Our prayers chase our lives. The shape of our praying keeps adjusting to the shape of our lives.

The question, of course, is *"Why?"* Why do we sometimes receive *whatever we ask* but not always? If God ever answers prayers for some, why not always for everyone, especially when people genuinely, sincerely, faithfully pray for the safety of their children or the healing of those they love or deliverance from crippling addictions? If prayers for trinkets and luxuries are not answered, we understand. But cries for deliverance or reconciliation? Earnest pleas for protection or healing? It's not that we become disillusioned with God or bitter or even angry when we do not receive those good things for which we pray, it's just that we are then left to wonder what those verses really mean, those *"whatever we ask"* Bible verses that always sound so simple on the page but sometimes seem less certain on the ground.

In her book *An Altar in the World*, Barbara Brown Taylor tells about a friend of hers who was losing a loved one to an early death. He was talking one day about his fervent prayers for God to step in and save the life of his dying loved one. When Reverend Taylor asked him if he believed God really would intervene with that kind of last-minute miracle, her friend replied, *"Honestly, I don't try to think all that through. I just tell God what I want. I'm not smart enough or strong enough to do anything else...I just tell God what I want and trust God to sort it all out."*[1] Those are among the best words about prayer I have ever heard: *"I just tell God what I want and trust God to sort it all out. I am not smart enough or strong enough to do anything but that."* Such truthful speech about prayer calls to memory what the Psalmist says in Psalm 42 about *deep calling to deep*. From the deepest depth of our hopes, fears, longings, and desires we call to the deepest depth of God's goodness, power, mercy, and love.[2] We don't look at prayer as some sort of transaction by which we convince God to come around and do our will. We don't think of prayer as another way for us to try and manage

---

[1] Barbara Brown Taylor, *An Altar in the World* (New York: Harper Collins, 2009) 182.

[2] This way of thinking about Psalm 42:7 is one I first heard in a prayer by Jill Barnes Buckley.

God or control our lives. We just call to the depths of God's love from the depths of our lives, because we know we are not smart enough or strong enough to do anything other than that.

Amen.

AWFUL AND WONDERFUL

A Psalm of David. [1]The Lord is my shepherd, I shall not want. [2]He makes me lie down in green pastures; he leads me beside still waters; [3]He restores my soul. He leads me in right paths for his name's sake.

[4] Even though I walk through the darkest valley, I fear no evil; for you are with me; Your rod and your staff—they comfort me.

[5]You prepare a table before me in the presence of my enemies; you anoint my head with oil; my cup overflows. [6]Surely goodness and mercy shall follow me all the days of my life, and I shall dwell in the house of the Lord my whole life long. —Psalm 23

Over near the end of Thornton Wilder's Pulitzer Prize-winning play *Our Town*, there is that brief scene in which we get to listen in on a conversation among some people who have long been dead. From their vantage point up in what Wilder calls "*The land of the dead*," they are looking down on the funeral of a bright and wonderful young woman when one of them, a lady named Mrs. Soames, says that she had forgotten just how painful life could be, which leads her to observe, "*My, wasn't life awful*." Then, after a long pause, she adds, "*And wonderful*."[1]

"*Wasn't life awful....And wonderful*." As sentences go, that one is very fine and very true. In fact, Mrs. Soames' observation that life was both awful and wonderful sounds a lot like something you sometimes see in the Psalms. Take

---

[1] Thornton Wilder, *Our Town* (New York: Harper and Row, 1938) 86.

Psalm 13, for example. In verse 2, life is awful: "*How long must I bear pain in my soul?*" but by verse 6 life is wonderful: "*I will sing to the Lord, because the Lord has been good to me.*" Then there is Psalm 18, where life is awful in verse 4, "*The pains of death surrounded me*" and wonderful in verse 19, "*The Lord supported me and brought me out to a good place.*" In Psalm 22, life is awful in verse 1, "*My God, my God, why have you forsaken me?*" and wonderful in verse 24, "*God did not hide from me, but heard me when I cried.*" It happens again in Psalm 55, where life is awful in verse 4, "*My heart is in anguish*" and wonderful in verse eighteen, "*God will redeem me unharmed from the battle I must wage*"—not to mention Psalm 63, where life is awful in verse 1, "*My soul thirsts and faints in a dry and weary land,*" and wonderful in verse 5, "*My soul is satisfied with a rich feast and my mouth praises God with joyful lips.*" And then, of course, there is the all-time, number-one, most-loved Psalm of all, where awful and wonderful sit side by side—not just in the same Psalm, but in the same sentence. The sentence at the center of Psalm 23 starts out awful: "*In the valley of the shadow of death,*" and ends up wonderful: "*Fearing no evil,*" comforted and cared for by God the good shepherd.

When the Psalmist talks about going "*Through the valley of the shadow of death,*" he is speaking a language we understand. We get that, because we've done that. We are not strangers to those deep, dark, long, exhausting valleys that must be gone through because they cannot be gotten around. There is a long list of ways things can go wrong in this life. None of us will go through all of them, but all of us will go through some of them, and the worst of them will leave us saying with the Psalmist that we are walking, "*Through the valley of the shadow of death.*"

If you've been there, you know how awful it can be, but you also know that even when life is that awful, there's also something wonderful about the way God journeys with us through the awfulness. *"Even though I walk through the valley of the shadow of death, I will fear no evil, because God is with me and God comforts me."* That's the way the Psalmist said it. And it's true. Even when we're going through the most awful valleys, God is still doing the most wonderful things. Even when some parts of our lives are awful because God didn't keep us out of the terrible valley, other parts of our lives are wonderful because God is going through the terrible valley with us.

All of this raises a question: *If God is that involved with us in the awful valley, why didn't God just shepherd us around the awful valley in the first place?* Apparently, life does not work that way. Not always, anyway. Sometimes, perhaps, but not always. Of course, that raises the additional question, *If God sometimes protects some of us from some awful things, why doesn't God always protect all of us from all awful things?* I don't know. I am frequently reminded of what William Sloane Coffin said after the tragic death of his young son: *"This time God gave us minimum protection and maximum support."*[2] The Coffin family didn't get enough protection to take them around the valley of the shadow of death, but they did get enough support to take them through it, which has also been the experience of many of us.

"Life was awful," said the woman in the play, *"Wasn't life awful...and wonderful."* And she was right...twice. It's awful what we have to go through in this life, and it's wonderful the way God, and God's people, go through it with us.

Somehow, God gives us the strength to go through things that, had someone told us ahead of time we were going to have to go through, we would have sworn we could not endure. But

---

[2] *A Cloud of Witnesses*, ed. Thomas G. Long and Cornelius Platinga (Grand Rapids: Eerdmans, 1994).

we do go through; we do, we have, and we will. By the grace of God, and with the people of God, we do go through.

Amen.

WRESTLING, STRUGGLING, STRIVING, LIMPING

[22]That same night he got up and took his two wives, his two maids, and his eleven children, and crossed the ford of the Jabbok. [23]He took them and sent them across the stream, and likewise everything that he had. [24]Jacob was left alone; and a man wrestled with him until daybreak. [25]When the man saw that he did not prevail against Jacob, he struck him on the hip socket; and Jacob's hip was put out of joint as he wrestled with him. [26]Then he said, "Let me go, for the day is breaking." But Jacob said, "I will not let you go, unless you bless me." [27]So he said to him, "What is your name?" And he said, "Jacob." [28]Then the man said, "You shall no longer be called Jacob, but Israel, for you have striven with God and with humans, and have prevailed." [29]Then Jacob asked him, "Please tell me your name." But he said, "Why is it that you ask my name?" And there he blessed him. [30]So Jacob called the place Peniel, saying, "For I have seen God face to face, and yet my life is preserved." [31]The sun rose upon him as he passed Penuel, limping because of his hip. —Genesis 32:22–31

Ever since the night of the fight, he's not been quite the same. I'm talking about Jacob. Before the awful night of the terrible fight, Jacob was always up to something.... Taking advantage of his hungry brother, deceiving his aging father, out-foxing his father-in-law in a perpetual game of one-upmanship. For Jacob, nothing was ever enough and, in the endless quest for more, he seemed always to have something else up his sleeve.

But then there came that crisis in his life, that night when Jacob knew that the next face he saw was going to belong to Esau. All those years ago when Jacob took Esau's blessing from their father, Esau swore that someday he would make Jacob pay. In Genesis chapter 32, that long-promised payday is scheduled for the next day. So now there's nowhere to turn, no place to go, nothing to do. It's just Jacob and God; wrestling, struggling, and striving the way we all do when we're consumed with fear and dread because we're up against something we can't manage or change or conquer.

So, all through the night, Jacob tosses and turns and struggles and strives, wrestling with his fears and his guilt, his past and his future, his demons and himself and God. It's got to be the longest, darkest, worst night of his life. But if you read Jacob's whole story, from his birth in Genesis 25 to his death in chapter 49, you get the impression that the worst night he ever endured was also the best blessing he ever received. When the sun comes up, Jacob is still the same person, but he is also somehow different. For one thing, he's been given new name. And then there's the limp. Back in the day, Jacob was so smooth and smart and proud he could "strut sitting down." But not now. Now he has this bad limp. He's a little slower now. And when you read the rest of his story, he seems a little less arrogant, a little more content. He's the same, but he's not the same, ever since the long night of the big fight.

Why does it so often seem to work that way? Why does it almost always take a crisis to strip us down and open us up and get us real with God? Why is it that most of the real progress we make in holiness and humility are the gains that come from our losses and our struggles? Doing well and flying high are fine, but they rarely help us get on, and stay on, the path to depth. Only pain, fear, and struggle, it seems, can drive us deeper into humility and holiness and take us farther on the path to depth. Why does the path to depth seem always to take us into and through deep darkness and great struggle?

So don't fear the struggle, and don't give up. Hold on and fight through. Say to your struggle what Jacob said to his: *I will not let you go until you bless me.* You may emerge from the awful struggle so changed by it that, like Jacob, you may as well have a new name.

And maybe, if all goes well, you'll never get over it. You'll get through it, but hopefully not over it. Hopefully you'll spend the rest of your life as a deeper, quieter, kinder child of God, limping a little from the struggle that changed you, made you better, and left you a little more redeemed than you ever would have been had you never known the darkness.

Amen.

HOW LONG WILL WE GRIEVE?

¹⁶The Lord said to Samuel, "How long will you grieve over Saul? I have rejected him from being king over Israel. Fill your horn with oil and set out; I will send you to Jesse the Bethlehemite, for I have provided for myself a king among his sons." ²Samuel said, "How can I go? If Saul hears of it, he will kill me." And the Lord said, "Take a heifer with you, and say, 'I have come to sacrifice to the Lord.' ³Invite Jesse to the sacrifice, and I will show you what you shall do; and you shall anoint for me the one whom I name to you." ⁴Samuel did what the Lord commanded, and came to Bethlehem. The elders of the city came to meet him trembling, and said, "Do you come peaceably?" ⁵He said, "Peaceably; I have come to sacrifice to the Lord; sanctify yourselves and come with me to the sacrifice." And he sanctified Jesse and his sons and invited them to the sacrifice.

⁶When they came, he looked on Eliab and thought, "Surely the Lord's anointed is now before the Lord." ⁷But the Lord said to Samuel, "Do not look on his appearance or on the height of his stature, because I have rejected him; for the Lord does not see as mortals see; they look on the outward appearance, but the Lord looks on the heart." ⁸Then Jesse called Abinadab, and made him pass before Samuel. He said, "Neither has the Lord chosen this one." ⁹Then Jesse made Shammah pass by. And he said, "Neither has the Lord chosen this one." ¹⁰Jesse made seven of his sons pass before Samuel, and Samuel said to Jesse, "The Lord has not chosen any of these." ¹¹Samuel said to Jesse, "Are all your sons here?" And he said, "There remains yet the youngest, but he is keeping the sheep." And Samuel said to Jesse, "Send and bring him; for we will not sit down until he comes here." ¹²He sent and brought him in. Now he was

ruddy, and had beautiful eyes, and was handsome. The Lord said, "Rise and anoint him; for this is the one." [13]Then Samuel took the horn of oil, and anointed him in the presence of his brothers; and the spirit of the Lord came mightily upon David from that day forward. Samuel then set out and went to Ramah. —1 Samuel 16:1–13

Samuel needs a little more time. God is ready for Samuel to go find the next king, but Samuel hasn't finished grieving over the last one. So, God waits as long as God can, until finally God says, *"Samuel, how long will you grieve over Saul, since I have rejected him from being king over Israel? Fill your horn with oil, and go; I will send you to Jesse the Bethlehemite, for I have selected a king for myself from among his sons."*

And, over the next few verses, Samuel does just that. He gets back to work. He tends to the things for which he is responsible. But, he never answers the question. He goes and does what God tells him, but he never answers God's question about how long he will grieve; a silence that comes as no surprise to us, because, as everyone who has ever grieved anything knows, *"How long will you grieve?"* is a question for which there is no good answer. The waves of grief come when they come, for as long as they come. They come when we expect them; but they also come rolling in out of the blue, washing over us with no warning and seemingly for no reason. So, of course, Samuel couldn't say how long he would grieve over Saul, because no one can say how long they will grieve over anyone or anything.

Plus, Saul was still alive, which added a layer of complexity to Samuel's grief. God had rejected Saul as king, but Saul was still alive and on the throne. So, Samuel was grieving over something he could not put behind him, because it was still in front of him. Samuel's grief wasn't over because

Samuel's pain wasn't over, which may be the most complicated grief of all, the lingering grief of unresolved disappointment and unfinished pain.

But Samuel had to live on, even if he wasn't ready to move on. Still deep in grief, Samuel packed his bags, headed for Bethlehem, and went back to work. Which, of course, is what we all do. We don't grieve, *then* get on with our lives. Rather, we grieve *and* go to work. We grieve *and* celebrate holidays. We grieve *and* sing in the choir. We grieve *and* dance at weddings. We grieve *and* do the next thing, whatever the next thing is. By the grace of God, and with the help of the people of God, we grieve *and* laugh and grieve *and* pray and grieve *and* sing and grieve *and* live; not first one and then the other, but both at the very same time in the very same, very deep breath—for as long as it takes, or as long as it lasts, or perhaps, if needed, for as long as we live.

Amen.

IF JUDAS HAD WAITED

[15]In those days Peter stood up among the believers (together the crowd numbered about one hundred and twenty people) and said, [16]"Friends, the scripture had to be fulfilled, which the Holy Spirit through David foretold concerning Judas, who became a guide for those who arrested Jesus— [17]for he was numbered among us and was allotted his share in this ministry." [18](Now this man acquired a field with the reward of his wickedness; and falling headlong, he burst open in the middle and all his bowels gushed out. [19]This became known to all the residents of Jerusalem, so that the field was called in their language Hakeldama, that is, Field of Blood.) [20]"For it is written in the book of Psalms, 'Let his homestead become desolate, and let there be no one to live in'; and 'Let another take his position of overseer.' [21]So one of the men who have accompanied us throughout the time that the Lord Jesus went in and out among us, [22]beginning from the baptism of John until the day when he was taken up from us—one of these must become a witness with us to his resurrection." [23]So they proposed two, Joseph called Barsabbas, who was also known as Justus, and Matthias. [24]Then they prayed and said, "Lord, you know everyone's heart. Show us which one of these two you have chosen [25]to take the place in this ministry and apostleship from which Judas turned aside to go to his own place." [26]And they cast lots for them, and the lot fell on Matthias; and he was added to the eleven apostles. Acts 1:15–26

One imagines that convening that meeting might have felt a bit awkward for Peter. I'm talking about that meeting in Acts chapter 1, the meeting Peter convened for the purpose of replacing Judas. That might have been at least a little awkward for Peter, given the fact that Judas was being replaced for betraying Jesus—a serious sin, but a sin no more serious than Peter's own. After all, the same night Judas betrayed Jesus, Peter denied Jesus. At the moment when Jesus needed them most, Judas and Peter performed equally poorly. One failed about as badly as the other. The main difference between Peter and Judas was that Peter lived to see the risen Lord, so he found a second chance and made a new beginning, whereas Judas, on the other hand, was not around to see the risen Lord. According to the gospel of Matthew, Judas sank into such a deep despair over what he had done that he chose to end his misery by ending his life.

I've often wondered what might have happened if Judas had held on just a little longer. If only Judas had waited. Since Judas' failure was no worse than Peter's, one can only assume that had Judas waited he would have received the same second chance Peter received from the risen Lord. If Judas had waited, one imagines that he, too, would have been forgiven, restored, and given a new beginning. If only Judas had waited, who knows how things might have turned out? But, apparently, Judas sank to such a depth of despair that he decided his life would never again be livable or bearable, and in that tragic moment he made the tragic choice to end his own life.

I cannot think of Judas' death without thinking of others who, like Judas, found the pain of life so unbearable that they sought relief in death, leaving their families to live with the deep and complex grief that follows the death of a loved one who ended their own life; a deep and complex grief for which the church should have a tender word of grace and hope. The most helpful and truthful words I have ever heard about the sorrow of suicide were spoken by the late dean of Westminster

Abbey, the Reverend Michael Mayne. When Mayne was four years old, his dad, the pastor of a small British Anglican church, climbed to the top of a bell tower and leaped to his death. Seventy years later, Michael Mayne, by then a distinguished pastor and theologian, reflected on his dad's death with these remarkable words: *"We shall never know why you did what you did, for that is known only to you and God. But we do know that your desperate cry for help came out of so much unrecognizable anguish of spirit that it demands, not our judgment, but our compassion. One thing your action has taught me is that none of us really understands the heart of another human being, and none of us dare pass judgment on the life or death of another. That is God's prerogative, for God alone perfectly understands, and God's judgment is always more than matched by God's mercy."*[1]

Those may be the truest and best words anyone could possibly say concerning those whose grief or fear or despair or darkness became so deep that they sought relief in death. When someone we love makes that choice, it isn't our fault or anybody's fault. There is no blame to lay, just pain to bear. If only they had waited for light to break or things to change or hope to return. But they didn't, perhaps because, for a tragic moment, they thought they couldn't. Because I believe with the apostle Paul that no kind of life and no kind of death will be able to separate us from the love of God, I also believe that souls so heavily burdened and unbearably troubled in this life are received by God in the next life with healing mercy and the eternal embrace of God's love and grace.

You will perhaps remember, from the gospel accounts of the final night of Jesus' life, that the last time Jesus and Judas were together, Judas kissed Jesus. In his book *Peculiar*

---

[1] This passage is borrowed from a sermon by Michael Mayne.

Treasures,[2] Frederick Buechner imagines that the next time they saw one another, Jesus kissed Judas.

Amen.

---

[2] Frederick Buechner, *Peculiar Treasures* (San Francisco: Harper, 1979) 94.

THE WAY GOD IS

^{20}Early on the first day of the week, while it was still dark, Mary Magdalene came to the tomb and saw that the stone had been removed from the tomb. ^{2}So she ran and went to Simon Peter and the other disciple, the one whom Jesus loved, and said to them, "They have taken the Lord out of the tomb, and we do not know where they have laid him." ^{3}Then Peter and the other disciple set out and went towards the tomb. ^{4}The two were running together, but the other disciple outran Peter and reached the tomb first. ^{5}He bent down to look in and saw the linen wrappings lying there, but he did not go in. ^{6}Then Simon Peter came, following him, and went into the tomb. He saw the linen wrappings lying there, ^{7}and the cloth that had been on Jesus' head, not lying with the linen wrappings but rolled up in a place by itself. ^{8}Then the other disciple, who reached the tomb first, also went in, and he saw and believed; ^{9}for as yet they did not understand the scripture, that he must rise from the dead. ^{10}Then the disciples returned to their homes. —John 20:1–10

By the time we get to Easter, God has already had a long career of, in the words of Carlyle Marney, *"taking what looks like the end of everything good, and turning it into the edge of something new."* When God raised Jesus from the grave, that did not indicate some new, more New Testament, Christian development in God's character. God had always been that kind of God, the kind of God whose love, grace, and goodness had always found a way to triumph and prevail over sin, separation, pain, and death.

It started early, all the way back in Eden, where God told Adam and Eve that, on the day they ate from the off-limits tree, they would die. They did eat, but they did not die. Instead, God gave them sturdier clothes to help them make it in the rougher world they had created for themselves. Then, in Genesis chapter 6, verse 7, God said, *"It's hopeless. I'm wiping out the whole creation; people, animals, everything. No exceptions. It's over."* But in the very next verse, Genesis 6:8, Noah found grace in the sight of the Lord. In Isaiah chapter 10, things were so bad that God said, of God's people, *"I will make a full end of you,"* but in Jeremiah chapter 31 the same God tells the same people to tune up their tambourines and line up for a line-dance, because God loves them with a relentless and everlasting love. In Hosea chapter 4, God says to God's people, *"You have wandered so far for so long that I am now officially declaring you forgotten and rejected,"* but in Hosea chapter 11, the same God says the same people, *"How can I give you up? My heart won't let me let you go."* And, in Zephaniah chapter 1, God said, *"It's really over this time. This time, I'm wiping everybody and everything off the planet."* But, two pages later, the same God says to the same people, *"Sing aloud, O daughter Zion, rejoice and be glad with all your heart. The Lord your God is with you, and I will bring you home."*

So when God raised Jesus from the grave, that was just God being God. God had always been that way; relentlessly loving, healing, and redeeming what is broken in this world and wrong in our lives; never giving up, always loving, healing, and redeeming what is broken beyond repair and too painful to bear. The resurrection is the ultimate sign of the relentless love and goodness of God—love and goodness that will stop at nothing and go through everything to see us through and bring us out.

Of course, we have to be careful here. The triumph of God's love and goodness over pain and death at Easter is not a sign that everything will work out and be fine in this life. To say this would be to say something that is not true, and people do not get up, get dressed, and go to church on Sunday morning to be told cheerful-sounding things that will not prove true in life's toughest arenas. Everything doesn't get changed or healed or redeemed or resolved in this world or in this life. But the resurrection of Christ from the grave is a sign that God's relentless love has all the time in the world; not just the time we have on this side of the grave, but the time God has on the other side of the grave. If the resurrection has truly robbed the grave of its power and victory, then God can love as relentlessly after death as God can love before death. (Oddly enough, it is we Christians, who sing *"Where thy victory, O Grave?"*, who are least willing to let God love and redeem as relentlessly after death as before death. Popular Christianity says God can love, redeem, and save relentlessly here but not there, now but not then. But, thanks be to God, not even twenty centuries of orthodox Christian doctrine can tell God when to quit saving and stop redeeming.) The resurrection of Jesus from the grave is the ultimate sign of the relentless love of God, the love that never gives up, quits, stops, or goes away; the great, relentless love of God that ultimately, finally, will "take what looked like the end of everything good and turn it into the edge of something new."[1]

If life has been kind to you and you have been kind to life, if you've been lucky enough and smart enough to make all the right choices, so that you are easy for God to love and welcome, all this talk of God's relentless love may not mean so much to you. But if you have come to the empty tomb as Mary

---

[1] This is a phrase I heard attributed to Carlyle Marney.

came, *in the dark*, if you have come broken or guilty, ashamed or angry, fighting hard battles and filled with self-doubt, self-loathing, uncertainty, and fear, then hear the good news, the glad good Easter news that the God you have is the God you need, and the God you need is the God you have—the never-gives-up, never-goes-away, never-lets-go God who has a long career of loving *relentlessly*.

    Amen.

FOR THIS LIFE ONLY?

[12]Now if Christ is proclaimed as raised from the dead, how can some of you say there is no resurrection of the dead? [13]If there is no resurrection of the dead, then Christ has not been raised; [14]and if Christ has not been raised, then our proclamation has been in vain and your faith has been in vain. [15]We are even found to be misrepresenting God, because we testified of God that he raised Christ—whom he did not raise if it is true that the dead are not raised. [16]For if the dead are not raised, then Christ has not been raised. [17]If Christ has not been raised, your faith is futile and you are still in your sins. [18]Then those also who have died in Christ have perished. [19]If for this life only we have hoped in Christ, we are of all people most to be pitied.

[20]But in fact Christ has been raised from the dead, the first fruits of those who have died. [21]For since death came through a human being, the resurrection of the dead has also come through a human being; [22]for as all die in Adam, so all will be made alive in Christ. [23]But each in his own order: Christ the first fruits, then at his coming those who belong to Christ. [24]Then comes the end, when he hands over the kingdom to God the Father, after he has destroyed every ruler and every authority and power. [25]For he must reign until he has put all his enemies under his feet. [26]The last enemy to be destroyed is death. —1 Corinthians 15:12–26

It would appear that, when it comes to Easter, Paul has a tendency to put all his eggs in one basket. When it comes to the resurrection, as far as Paul is concerned, it's *all or nothing*: If Christ has been raised from death, all is well. But, if not, nothing else matters. That's what Paul says about the resurrection in 1 Corinthians chapter 15, and he says it with *all or nothing* finality when he declares, first in verse 14 and again in verse 17, *"If Christ has not been raised, our faith is pointless."* And then, as if that wasn't enough, in verse 18 Paul says that if Christ has not been raised, then death was the end for Jesus, and if death was the end for Jesus, then death will also be the end for us. All of which is followed, in verse 19, by the most *all or nothing* pronouncement Paul can muster: *"If for this life only we have hoped in Christ, we are of all people most to be pitied."*

I know that when Paul says, *"If for this life only we have hoped in Christ, we are of all people most to be pitied,"* he is invoking extreme language to make an important point, but careful speech requires me to say that I don't know about the pity part of that verse. At the end of the day, when all is said and done, if I should discover that I had trusted in Christ for this life only, I wouldn't want to be pitied. If I discovered that I had trusted in Christ for this life only, I'd say, *"Don't cry for me. Loving God and living for Jesus, praying, singing, serving the church, and believing the gospel, is the greatest life in the world. Even if I knew it was for this life only, I wouldn't change a thing."*

But, of course, all that's beside the point, because the fact is, our hope in Christ is *not* for this life only because Christ *has* been raised and death *has* been defeated and there *is* life beyond the grave. That's what we believe. And beyond that, not only do we believe there is life beyond the grave, we also believe that the life that waits on *that* side of the grave is better than the life we know on *this* side of the grave. We believe that all that is broken here will be mended there. We believe that deep wounds that could not be healed in *this* life will be healed in *that* life, because we believe that God is actually going to do God's best work over on the other side. We know that, on *this* side of the grave, the blind don't see and the lame don't walk, but we believe they will on *that* side of the grave because we believe that there is no good and beautiful thing God cannot, and will not, do, over on the other side.

Except for one thing. We have been taught to believe that, beyond the grave, over on the other side, God can do anything wonderful God wants to do except for one thing, which is to give redeeming grace to someone who failed to receive it in this life. We have been taught to believe that, beyond the grave, God can and will heal the sick, restore the broken, repair the damaged, and relieve the depressed, but we are not supposed to believe God can give redeeming grace beyond the grave because that would require some kind of opportunity after death to respond to the mercy of God, and we have always been taught that the opportunity to receive God's grace is for this life only, so we have always believed that the possibility of redemption runs out at the grave.

Of all the things we've always been taught, I cannot think of anything I'd rather someday find out we were wrong about than that. I cannot imagine how wonderful it would be to someday find out, over on the other side, that, despite what popular Christianity says we should believe, God is as free to love, redeem, and forgive on the other side of the grave as God is free to love, redeem, and forgive on this side of the grave.

Wouldn't you love to someday find out that grace is greater than the grave? I'd love to someday find out that, all this time, we've been wrong, thinking that death has enough power to stop God from doing what God does best, which is to redeem, save, welcome, and embrace.

Well, yeah, but what about that verse in Luke where Father Abraham tells the rich man in hell it's too late for him to cross over to the good and happy side? And isn't there also a verse in there somewhere that talks about people knocking on the door after it's too late to come in? Indeed, those verses are in the Bible, and they do call us with all urgency to decide today, while the opportunity is ours, to give ourselves to the life-transforming gospel of God. And, when death comes, our opportunity to choose that grace-filled, gospel-transformed life, will end. Our opportunity to choose God's grace in this life will end with our last heartbeat. But does that mean God gives up, just because we had our last heartbeat? Does death really have that much power over God, even now that death has been defeated by the resurrection? God's love, defeated by death? God's will, defeated by the grave? I don't think so.

Here's something to think about: What if, all this time, we've been overestimating death because we've been underestimating Easter? What if the resurrection has so completely conquered death that death not only can't keep God from giving sight to the blind beyond the grave, it also can't keep God from giving grace to the lost beyond the grave? *But that's not what we're supposed to believe.* I know, I know. But wouldn't it be wonderful to someday find out we were wrong? (Because, if we're not wrong, if we're right when we say there's no grace beyond the grave, that means that death is going to have the last word, and that would mean that the last enemy, death, has not been overcome by Easter after all, not if death has the power to eternally stop God from doing what God does best.)

Don't you hope we're wrong when we say there is no grace beyond the grave? (I do. I hope we're wrong, and I believe we are.) Wouldn't you love to someday discover that, all this time, we've been *overestimating* death and *underestimating* Easter?

Amen.

I'M GLAD I DID THAT

⁶As for me, I am already being poured out as a libation, and the time of my departure has come. ⁷I have fought the good fight, I have finished the race, I have kept the faith. ⁸From now on there is reserved for me the crown of righteousness, which the Lord, the righteous judge, will give to me on that day, and not only to me but also to all who have longed for his appearing. —2 Timothy 4:6–8

I believe that the essence of living is this; to come to the brink of death, look back across your life, and say with a solid smile, "I'm glad I did that."[1] A few years after writing those words, the famous humorist Grady Nutt lost his life in a sudden and tragic accident, so we will never know if, on the day of his death, he had time to look back across his life, and say, with a solid smile, *"I'm glad I did that."* But it does appear that the writer of 2 Timothy had such a moment, an *"I'm glad I did that"* moment that is captured in those beautiful old words, *"The time of my departure has come. I have fought the good fight. I have finished the race. I have kept the faith."*

It would be wonderful if we could all face our own death with that much peace about our life. Of course, in order for us to die that way, we would first have to live that way. In order to die saying, *"The time of my departure has come. I have fought the good fight, I have finished the race, I have kept the faith,"* we would first have to have lived a *"keep the faith"* kind of life——a life punctuated by moments, words, choices, and decisions about which we could truly say, *"I'm glad I did that."*

---

[1] I heard this story in a sermon by Walter Shurden.

The problem, of course, is that no one can say *"I'm glad I did that"* about every moment of their life. Our lives are flawed, our motives are mixed, and we all suffer from our own fair share of the countless complexities of the human condition. We sin. We fail. Even Saint Paul, to whom this passage is traditionally attributed, would not have been able to say *"I'm glad I did that"* about all of his life, or perhaps even most of his life. After all, he was, early on, a violent persecutor who denied people their religious freedom. And, even after he had been a Christian a long, long time, Paul wrote in Romans chapter 7 his great lament, *"I do the things I know I shouldn't, and the things I know I should do I don't do."* Even Paul had his demons, fought his battles, faced his own dilemmas. Paul certainly could not have said *"I'm glad I did that"* about everything he knew about himself. And yet, tradition has long held that, though 1 and 2 Timothy may have been composed by a next-generation follower of Paul's, these deathbed words are Paul's words— Paul's way of looking back at the best of his life from the brink of his death and saying, with a solid smile, *"I'm glad I did that: I've fought the fight. I've run the race. I've kept the faith. I'm ready to go."*

What a way to die. Or, more to the point, what a way to live. Viktor Frankl once wrote, *"Project yourself onto your own deathbed. Now, from that vantage point, what do you wish you had done with your life?"*[2] I stumbled across that sentence when I was about thirty years old. It stopped me in my tracks then, and it still does now. *"Project yourself onto your own deathbed. Now, from that vantage point, what do you wish you had done with your life?"* If you were on your deathbed today, right now, would there be a conversation you wish you had had? A letter you wish you had written? An apology you wish you had

---

[2] Source unknown.

made? A stand you wish you had taken? A forgiveness you wish you had sought from someone or given to someone? Project yourself onto your own deathbed. Are you there? Good. Now, from that vantage point, what do you wish you had done with your life?

If I were on my deathbed today I would wish I had not allowed my fears to so dominate my life. The landscape of my life is so littered with failures of courage that my version of Paul's benediction would have to be, *"The time of my departure is at hand. I have fought the fight (tentatively), run the race (cautiously), and kept the faith (timidly)."* What about you? When you project yourself onto your deathbed, what do you wish you had done differently? If you were there now, what would be your great regret? On the other hand, what would make you glad? As surely as we all have our regrets, our remorse, our moments we wish we could have back, we all also have moments that, when we look back on them, cause us to say, with a solid smile, *"I'm glad I did that."* For most of us, those are small moments of kindness or truth or both—the important conversations we did have, the true words we did say, the overdue visits we did make, the brave stands we did take, moments of kindness or truth or courage or faith that cause us to say, with a solid smile, *"I'm glad I did that."* I had a moment like that when the church in Florida was planning to hold a "Burn the Koran" day. I watched all that for as long as I could without doing anything. But, eventually, that old Baptist gene got the best of me, and I found myself downtown on Pascagoula Street, walking in the door of the International Museum of Muslim Culture. I went in and asked to see the director. I told her I was a Baptist preacher and that I was there to ask her forgiveness on behalf of Christians whose conduct did not embody the spirit of God. We prayed together and then I left. It was the smallest of gestures. It took less than fifteen minutes of my day. But, that night when I lay my head on my pillow, I looked up toward the sky and said, *"Lord, I'm glad I did that."*

You often have that experience, don't you? Of course you do. You listen to the Spirit. You take a few moments to make the call or write the note. Or you take the gospel step that feels awkward. You get outside yourself in a way that is very uncomfortable to you and very pleasing to God. And then, at the end of the day, when it's just you and God, when you lie down to sleep, or, someday, at the end of the day, when you lie down to die, you are able to look back on that moment and say, with a solid smile, *"I'm glad I did that."*

Sisters and brothers, someday will be the last day. It would be a very good and beautiful thing, if, on the last day, we were able to say, *"I fought the fight. I ran the race. I kept the faith. I'm glad I did that."* The only way we'll be able to die that way, *then,* is for us to go ahead and live that way, *now.*

Amen.

OUR PATCHWORK QUILT OF HOPE

⁹After this I looked, and there was a great multitude that no one could count, from every nation, from all tribes and peoples and languages, standing before the throne and before the Lamb, robed in white, with palm branches in their hands. ¹⁰They cried out in a loud voice, saying, "Salvation belongs to our God who is seated on the throne, and to the Lamb!" ¹¹And all the angels stood around the throne and around the elders and the four living creatures, and they fell on their faces before the throne and worshipped God, ¹²singing, "Amen! Blessing and glory and thanksgiving and honour and power and might be to our God for ever and ever! Amen."

¹³Then one of the elders addressed me, saying, "Who are these, robed in white, and where have they come from?" ¹⁴I said to him, "Sir, you are the one that knows." Then he said to me, "These are they who have come out of the great ordeal; they have washed their robes and made them white in the blood of the Lamb. ¹⁵For this reason they are before the throne of God, and worship him day and night within his temple, and the one who is seated on the throne will shelter them. ¹⁶They will hunger no more, and thirst no more; sun will not strike them, nor any scorching heat; ¹⁷for the Lamb at the centre of the throne will be their shepherd, and he will guide them to springs of the water of life, and God will wipe away every tear from their eyes." Revelation 7:9–17

After this I looked, and there was a great multitude that no one could count, standing before the throne, robed in white and singing, "Blessing and glory, wisdom and honor be to our God forever and ever!... And the one on the throne will shelter them, and God will wipe every tear from their eyes." Those wonderful words from

Revelation chapter 7 are part of John's message of hope for his community of faith; late-first-century believers who were undergoing persecution at the hands of the Roman emperor Domitian; weary souls to whom John wrote in an effort to encourage them to remain faithful and be strong.

That means, of course, that those words from Revelation, like all the other words in Revelation, were not written about us. But that doesn't keep them from speaking to us. When the book of Revelation speaks of those who have gone through a great ordeal eventually being comforted by God, we see our faces in that crowd, because we believe that, over on the other side, God will wipe every tear from our eyes, too. In that sense, this passage from Revelation is not unlike those equally familiar words from Revelation chapter 21, *Then I saw a new heaven and a new earth. And I heard a loud voice from the throne saying, "The home of God is among people. God will be with them, and God will wipe every tear from their eyes, and sorrow and crying and pain and death will be no more."* That passage, too, was written to give comfort and hope to John's late-first-century community of faith, but that doesn't keep us from finding our own hope and comfort in it every time we hear it read at a funeral or near a grave.

The same is true for other passages. Take Isaiah 35, for example: *"The eyes of the blind will be opened and the ears of the deaf unstopped. The lame shall leap like a deer and the tongue of the speechless shall sing for joy, and sorrow and sighing shall flee away."* We know that Isaiah wrote those words not about us but about the return of the people of God to their homeland at the end of the exile, but that doesn't keep us from hearing in Isaiah's words the hope that someday our sorrow and sighing will flee away. Same with John 14:2, *"In my Father's house are many dwelling places. If it were not so, would I have told you that I go to prepare a place for you?"* and 2 Corinthians 5:1, *"We know that if this earthly tent in which we live be destroyed, we have a building from God, a house not made with hands, eternal in the heavens."* We know that those words were all originally written to, and for, someone else, but we have claimed them as our own and pieced them together into our own hope for relief, comfort, and joy over on the other side, in the next life, beyond the grave. Our hope of heaven is sort of like one of those beautiful old patchwork quilts that are pieced together by taking many small squares of cloth and stitching them together into one big, beautiful blanket. We have this wonderful, restful, joyful hope for life on the other side that we have pieced together from a verse here and a sentence there—a beautiful patchwork quilt of hope, hope for a day when, finally, eternally, endlessly, all will be well.

And, this side of the grave, that's about the best we can do. When it comes to our hope concerning life over on the other side, a pieced-together patchwork of verses and visions, words and dreams, scriptures and longings is probably about the best we can do. After all, we don't know what it's like to leave this life and go over on the other side. *Where is heaven? Is it up? Is it a physical place or a state of being? Will we know one another there? Can those who are already there see those of us who are still here?* These things we do not and cannot know. The truth is, we all believe about heaven what we choose to believe about heaven. As for facts and answers, we don't have many. Instead, what we do have is this big, beautiful, pieced-together patchwork quilt of verses, voices, visions, and dreams. Over here is a patch from the Gospel of John, where Jesus said, *"You will have pain now, but you will have joy later, and no one will take your joy from you."* And over there is a piece from Romans where Paul declares, *"Nothing in all creation, neither life or death or anything else will be able to separate us from the love of God."* Over here we have Evelyn Underhill's beautiful declaration, *"The universe is safe for souls."*[1] Over there is that marvelous story Betty Tupper told Frank Tupper about a mystical moment in the final months of her terminal illness when, while praying to be delivered from her fear of death, she felt the presence of God embrace her in a very strong way and afterward said *"She heard children laughing over on the Other Side."*[2] And over there is that dream Fred Buechner had about his dad, who many years before had taken his life; a dream in which Fred Buechner's father spoke to him and said, *"Don't worry. I know plenty now, and it's all good."*[3]

You take a dream here and a voice there, a small patch of Revelation, a little scrap of John, a familiar verse here, an old hymn there, and, before you know it, you've stitched together a big, beautiful patchwork quilt of hope. You spend your whole life putting it all together so that, at the end of the day, when the time comes for you to lie down, you can wrap up in it and go to sleep, trusting that you will awaken to something wonderful over on the other side—because, at the end of the day, when all is said and done, if God is who we say and believe God is, the universe is safe for souls and God will wipe all the tears from our eyes and all will finally, eternally, be well.

Amen.

---

[1] This is a quote I heard attributed to Underhill in a sermon by Arthur Coliandro.

[2] Tupper, *A Scandalous Providence,* 437.

[3] Source unknown.

On Knowing the Will of God

⁶They went through the region of Phrygia and Galatia, having been forbidden by the Holy Spirit to speak the word in Asia. ⁷When they had come opposite Mysia, they attempted to go into Bithynia, but the Spirit of Jesus did not allow them; ⁸so, passing by Mysia, they went down to Troas. ⁹During the night Paul had a vision: there stood a man of Macedonia pleading with him and saying, "Come over to Macedonia and help us." ¹⁰When he had seen the vision, we immediately tried to cross over to Macedonia, being convinced that God had called us to proclaim the good news to them. ¹¹We set sail from Troas and took a straight course to Samothrace, the following day to Neapolis, ¹²and from there to Philippi, which is a leading city of the district of Macedonia and a Roman colony. We remained in this city for some days. ¹³On the sabbath day we went outside the gate by the river, where we supposed there was a place of prayer; and we sat down and spoke to the women who had gathered there. ¹⁴A certain woman named Lydia, a worshipper of God, was listening to us; she was from the city of Thyatira and a dealer in purple cloth. The Lord opened her heart to listen eagerly to what was said by Paul. ¹⁵When she and her household were baptized, she urged us, saying, "If you have judged me to be faithful to the Lord, come and stay at my home." And she prevailed upon us. —Acts 16:6–15

Poor Paul, all dressed up with no place to go! In verse 6 of Acts chapter 16, he tries to go preach the gospel in Asia, but the Holy Spirit won't let him. So, in verse 7, he sets out for Bithynia, but once again the Spirit blocks his path. Poor Paul! Plan A, Asia, falls through and then Plan B, Bithynia, also turns out to be a dead end.

That small corner of the book of Acts has long had a deep hold on my life, perhaps because its uncertain starts and stops so closely mirror my own lifelong struggle to discern the will of God. That struggle started early for me because I, like millions of other Bible Belt children, grew up under the influence of that "cultural Calvinism" which taught us that God had a specific blueprint all laid out for our lives, and if we didn't find and follow that blueprint, if we misread the plan and took the wrong job or moved to the wrong city, we would be "*out of God's will.*" This idea came to torment me: *What if I miss God's will? What if I misinterpret what I think God is telling me and make a choice that takes me outside the will of God?* (It never occurred to me that God would probably not create a specific blueprint for my life that I had to discover in order to be in God's will, only to hide that blueprint from me and then punish me for not finding it.)

I would like to help us find a better, deeper, truer way to think about the will of God. A first, modest step toward deeper thoughts about the will of God might be fewer words about the will of God. We live in a world where the phrase "God's will" gets used awfully freely. Something doesn't work out, and we say, "*It must not have been God's will.*" Or, we don't succeed at something, and we say, "*I thought it was God's will, but God closed the door.*" Or, we decide to move someplace and we tell our family, "*This is God's will,*" which, of course, it might be. Or, on the other hand, it could be ambition or discontentment or restlessness that is making us move. (When we moved from Macon, Georgia, to Washington, DC, Joshua was fourteen and Maria was ten, a terribly difficult time for a family to move. Somewhere in the midst of those hard days, I said, "*We have to make this move because it is God's will for me to be the pastor of the First Baptist Church of Washington, DC.*" Well, maybe. Or maybe it was just my own longing that was taking us there.) I sometimes wonder if God is not frequently amazed at the things for which *the will of God* is credited, blamed, and made responsible. The truth is, everything is not a God thing. Some things are human things; human choices and actions for which we don't get to shift the responsibility to *"the will of God."*

Perhaps one way for us to clear up our thinking about the will of God is to clean up our language about the will of God by asking ourselves the question, *"What does careful speech allow us to say about the will of God?"* Is it possible for us confidently to say what God's will is for our lives? I believe it is. In fact, I think I can tell you, here and now, what is the will of God for your life and mine. It's actually rather clear. Here it is: In Micah's words, God's will for you and for me is that we do justice, love mercy, and walk humbly with our God. In Jesus' words, God's will for my life, and yours, is that we each love the Lord our God with all our heart, soul, and mind, and that we love our neighbor as ourselves. In James' words, God's will for all of us is that we care for widows and orphans in their distress, and keep ourselves unstained by the world. That's the will of God. The will of God is that we live lives of integrity and compassion, innocence and kindness, truthfulness and love. As for where we live that life and what we do for a living and whether we buy that house or take that job or make that investment or start that business, well, there's probably not a blueprint with our name on it that has all that all spelled out.

Perhaps the best we can do is to listen and pray and think and wait on the Lord, and then do our best to be and do what we believe God has gifted and called us to be and do. But that doesn't mean that God has only one right plan for our lives. And it also doesn't mean that if we listen, pray, think, and wait on the Lord, life will turn out the way we hoped or wanted, dreamed, or imagined. Fred Buechner once famously and beautifully wrote, "*We find our calling at the place where our deep gladness meets the world's deep need.*"[1] That is a wonderful description of the call of God, but, the truth is, everyone doesn't get to live at the intersection of their deep gladness and the world's deep need. Sometimes, it just doesn't work out that way. We may have to make peace with the fact that we will always be quietly haunted by the tender ghosts of "not quite" and "almost." Our finest dream may have to be given a decent burial. Our souls may have to "reach a settlement with our lives."

I would like to say that God has this one perfect plan all laid out for us that we will surely find if we pray and seek sincerely. But, the truth is, our lives become the cumulative total of our choices, some of which we will get right and some of which we might not. We start out as children with the whole world open before us. Then, with each succeeding choice, that wide world narrows. To say "Yes" to one thing might be to say "No" to every other thing that follows. And then, finally, someday you stop and look back. You turn off the television, the computer, the iPhone, and the iPod, and, alone with your coffee or your lemonade or your cup of tea, there you sit, alone with your life, looking back. Perhaps what you see makes you say, like the main character in Wendell Berry's *Jayber Crow*, "*Looking back, it seems to me as though I have been following the path that was laid out for me, and I have this feeling, which never leaves me, that I have been led.*"[2] Or, on the other hand, what you see as you look back may call to your mind Thomas Merton's

---

[1] Frederick Buechner, *Listening to Your Life* (San Francisco: HarperCollins, 1992) 186.

[2] Wendell Berry, *Jayber Crow* (Washington DC: Counterpoint, 2000) 133.

unforgettable statement, *"It is some people's vocation to go through life choosing wrong."*[3]

Whether our lives look like Jayber Crow's right path or Thomas Merton's wrong road may have more to do with our own complex motivations and difficult choices than with the will of God, missed or found. The will of God is more about how we lived and served than where we went and worked. We may have missed our moment somewhere along the way. We may have missed a choice or an opportunity or a big decision, but if we're living prayerful, mindful, thoughtful, truthful, gentle, agendaless, innocent, spirit-filled, walls-down, arms-out lives of bone-deep integrity and unfailing compassion, we haven't missed the will of God.

Amen.

---

[3] This is a quote I heard attributed to Merton.

THE GRIEF OF GUILT

¹Happy are those whose transgression is forgiven, whose sin is covered. ²Happy are those to whom the LORD imputes no iniquity, and in whose spirit there is no deceit. ³While I kept silence, my body wasted away through my groaning all day long. ⁴For day and night your hand was heavy upon me; my strength was dried up as by the heat of summer. *Selah* ⁵Then I acknowledged my sin to you, and I did not hide my iniquity; I said, "I will confess my transgressions to the LORD," and you forgave the guilt of my sin. *Selah* ⁶Therefore let all who are faithful offer prayer to you; at a time of distress, the rush of mighty waters shall not reach them. ⁷You are a hiding place for me; you preserve me from trouble; you surround me with glad cries of deliverance. *Selah* ⁸I will instruct you and teach you the way you should go; I will counsel you with my eye upon you. ⁹Do not be like a horse or a mule, without understanding, whose temper must be curbed with bit and bridle, else it will not stay near you. ¹⁰Many are the torments of the wicked, but steadfast love surrounds those who trust in the Lord. ¹¹Be glad in the Lord and rejoice, O righteous, and shout for joy, all you upright in heart. —Psalm 32

"When I kept silence, my body wasted away through my groaning all day long. God's hand was heavy upon me and my strength was dried up as by the heat of summer. Then I acknowledged my sin to God, and God forgave the guilt of my sin." With those words the writer of Psalm 32 put a frame around *the grief of guilt*—that particularly painful sorrow we feel when we know in our hearts we are wrong; that complex, complicated sadness that is

part regret, part remorse, part self-doubt, and part self-hatred; the grief of guilt.

I cannot speak for you, but I sometimes think that guilt might be the worst grief of all. I would take almost any sorrow, sickness, or pain over the grief of guilt, partly because guilt is isolating in a way our other griefs are not. Guilt, unlike most other forms of grief, cuts us off. It makes us feel cut off from God because it takes away our confidence with God. I think that's what the Bible means when it says that if we have sin in our hearts God does not hear our prayers. It isn't that God won't hear our prayers when we are full of guilt. Rather, it is that we won't say our prayers when we're full of guilt because we don't think we have a right to say them. We think that, before God, we haven't a leg to stand on, so we fall silent, stop praying, and isolate ourselves from the God we are ashamed to face; this leaves us all alone in the awful grief of our guilt, because the same guilt that makes us fear facing God also makes us ashamed to face others. The thought that we have lost the respect of those we love, or that we have failed those who counted on us, causes us to draw down and bend over and grieve alone. And that's not even the worst of it. The worst of it is knowing that it's our fault. Is there anything worse than being responsible; than knowing that you are inescapably, inarguably, undeniably to blame? No wonder the Psalmist said, concerning the grief of guilt, "*When I kept silence, my body wasted away through my groaning all day long. Day and night, God's hand was heavy upon me and my strength dried up.*" The poor Psalmist. The poor Psalmist is finished.... *Dried up, drained out, done, over, gone, finished....*

...Almost. Almost finished, but not quite. The Psalmist is not quite finished. There is something else coming. There is a "then": *Then,* says the Psalmist, *I acknowledged my sin to God and*

I did not hide my iniquity. I said, "I will confess my transgressions to the Lord," and you forgave the guilt of my sin. Happy are those whose transgression is forgiven and in whose spirit there is no deceit. Wow. That was quick. The Psalmist came clean, spoke the truth, took responsibility, confessed his sin, and, basically, went from zero to happy in two verses.

If only it were that simple. If only we could put our guilt away as easily, down here on the ground, as the Psalmist put his away back there on the page. But, down here on the ground, it's not always so simple or easy to set aside our guilt. The pain our sin has caused has already been felt, and life doesn't come with a rewind button. So, of course, it's not quite as simple as it sounds in the psalm. When the Psalmist glides from the pain of guilt to the joy of innocence in the space of a single, simple confession, he is singing in shorthand, collapsing years of grief, loss, confession, and forgiveness into the span of a single song. But, even if the Psalmist's song is an abbreviated shorthand, it is shorthand for the greatest truth in all the world, the truth that our guilt is no match for God's grace. *If our greatest grief is guilt and God's greatest gift is grace, then our greatest grief is no match for God's greatest gift.* The depth of God's grace is deeper than the depth of our guilt. Or, as my friend Kirby Godsey once wrote, *"God will always let us leave, but God will never let us go."*[1] Or, as William Sloane Coffin once said, *"There is more mercy in God than there is sin in us."*[2] Or, as I once heard my old Hebrew professor John Durham say, *"God knows the facts about us, but God is not discouraged by the facts about us because God also knows the truth about us, and the truth about us is that we are God's beloved and cherished children, no*

---

[1] I heard Kirby Godsey say this in a sermon.
[2] William Sloane Coffin, *Credo* (Louisville: Westminster John Knox, 2005).

matter what the facts about us might be."[3] Or, to put it as simply as it can possibly be said, God doesn't love us because we are good; God loves us because *God* is good.

I know, it's not that simple. In the aftermath of our sins, there are amends to be made and apologies to be offered. There is forgiveness to be sought and responsibility to be taken. There are real changes to be embraced and new practices to be adopted. There is hard, even painful, work to be done. After all, as Barbara Brown Taylor has so wisely written; *It is easier and less painful for us to rely on God's forgiveness of our sins than it is for us to believe that God might support us in our effort to quit them. Most of us would rather say, "I'm sorry. I feel really awful about what I have done," than actually start doing things differently. We would rather learn to live with guilt than face the hard work of new life.*[4]

So, confessing our sin and receiving God's grace is not simple. There is hard work and heavy lifting and real changing to be done. But you have to start somewhere, and there's really nowhere else to start but at the beginning, by telling God the truth God already knows and trusting God to do what God does best; forgiving, healing, redeeming, and loving us; refusing to abandon us; refusing to leave us bent over and all alone, lost in the grief of guilt.

Amen

---

[3] I heard John Durham say this in a sermon.

[4] Adapted from Barbara Brown Taylor, *Speaking of Sin* (Boston: Cowley Publications, 2002) 46, 64.

SOME HAVE MORE TO FORGIVE THAN OTHERS

^{21}Then Peter came and said to him, "Lord, if another member of the church sins against me, how often should I forgive? As many as seven times?" ^{22}Jesus said to him, "Not seven times, but, I tell you, seventy-seven times. ^{23}"For this reason the kingdom of heaven may be compared to a king who wished to settle accounts with his slaves. ^{24}When he began the reckoning, one who owed him ten thousand talents was brought to him; ^{25}and, as he could not pay, his lord ordered him to be sold, together with his wife and children and all his possessions, and payment to be made. ^{26}So the slave fell on his knees before him, saying, 'Have patience with me, and I will pay you everything.' ^{27}And out of pity for him, the lord of that slave released him and forgave him the debt. ^{28}But that same slave, as he went out, came upon one of his fellow slaves who owed him a hundred denarii; and seizing him by the throat, he said, 'Pay what you owe.' ^{29}Then his fellow slave fell down and pleaded with him, 'Have patience with me, and I will pay you.' ^{30}But he refused; then he went and threw him into prison until he would pay the debt. ^{31}When his fellow slaves saw what had happened, they were greatly distressed, and they went and reported to their lord all that had taken place. ^{32}Then his lord summoned him and said to him, 'You wicked slave! I forgave you all that debt because you pleaded with me. ^{33}Should you not have had mercy on your fellow slave, as I had mercy on you?' ^{34}And in anger his lord handed him over to be tortured until he would pay his entire debt. ^{35}So my heavenly Father will also do to every one of you, if you do not forgive your brother or sister from your heart." —Matthew 18:21–35

Then Peter said to Jesus, "Lord, if another member of the church sins against me, how often should I forgive? As many as seven times?" But Jesus said to Peter, "Not seven times, but seventy-seven times." Every three years, the lectionary places in our path those words from Matthew's gospel, along with the accompanying parable of the ungrateful servant who, though he had been forgiven an enormous debt, was unwilling to forgive someone who owed him a small debt, a refusal to forgive that ultimately cost him his own forgiveness; all of which tells us that we, who have *received* forgiveness, must not refuse to *give* forgiveness. Some ancient manuscripts say that Jesus said we should forgive *seventy-seven* times, while others say *seventy times seven*, but in either case, the point is the same: *Just as we have been forgiven by God more times than can be counted, so must we forgive those who sin against us.*

Every three years, the lectionary places that passage in our path, and every three years it lands more heavily on some ears than on others, because some of us have more to forgive than others. Some of us, like myself, have never had much to forgive. We've known our share of sorrows, but most of our sorrows have been the normal, inevitable struggles and losses that are a part of every human life. So, for some of us, forgiveness has never been that hard because we've never had much to forgive. But, that has not been the case for all of us. Some of us have been deeply hurt or harmed along the way by someone else's words or deeds, which means that this passage, with its call for us to forgive others as God has forgiven us, lands much more heavily on some ears than on others, because some have more to forgive than others.

The longer I live the more convinced I become that forgiveness might well be the most complicated of all the spiritual disciplines, partly because forgiveness requires us to do the hard work of confrontation. Forgiveness is not a sweet, nice "live and let live" nonchalance that turns a blind eye and looks the other way, pretending that all is well and things are fine. Rather, once an injustice has been done, it cannot be forgiven until it has been named, confronted, and called what it is; and calling it what it is requires us to make real judgments, and to have unspeakably painful conversations, which is about as complicated, uncomfortable, risky, and hard as any work we will ever do—which is why so many of us spend so much of our lives running from it.

And then, to further complicate things, there's the whole matter of when to forgive. Ephesians 4:26 says, *"Don't let the sun go down on your wrath,"* but if you've ever been truly wronged or hurt, you know that, while the sun may not set on our wrath, many, many suns will set on our pain, and it's hard to forgive something before it has finished hurting. To forgive a hurt that is completely in the past is one thing, but to forgive something you still have to face and fear is another matter altogether. In one of my first churches, an elderly couple was attacked by a family member. A few hours after the assault, as we sat on the couch in their den, the couple looked at me and said, concerning their attacker, *"We feel so bad because we can't forgive him yet."* Looking at the bloody bundle of gauze and tape on the elderly man's forehead, I said, *"The time for that will come. But right now, all you can do is fear him and seek protection from him. The blood may need to dry before you can forgive him."* It's hard to forgive something before the blood has dried, while it's still happening, before it has been resolved, finished, and put to rest.

This is probably one reason why it's a good thing the church throughout the world declares sin forgiven every Lord's Day. That great worldwide liturgical gesture gives us a family of faith to declare forgiven, for us, those things we are not yet able to declare forgiven all by ourselves. Ten years ago, in the immediate aftermath of 9/11, a Methodist minister went to the Pentagon to offer whatever help he could give. A military officer who was helping with the search and rescue operation recognized the minister, went over to the crime scene barricade, and said, *"Preacher, I just want you to know I won't be coming back to church for a while. After what happened here to my friends and colleagues, it's going to be a long time before I can pray that prayer the church prays every week, the one about 'Forgive us our trespasses, as we forgive those who trespass against us.'"* To which the minister replied, *"Now is no time for you to be staying away from church. You come on to church, and when they get to that part of the prayer you can't pray, you just be quiet, and let the church pray it for you until you can pray it again."*[1] Sometimes, we have to let the church say it for us until we can say it for ourselves. Sometimes, we have to let the church declare forgiven what we cannot yet forgive, because some of us have more to forgive than others.

Matthew 18:21–35 calls us to a life of free-flowing forgiveness, mercy, and grace. Because some have more to forgive than others, I am trying to buy some time and create some room in that passage for those who have been most deeply wounded and, thus, have the most to forgive. The danger in that, of course, is that we will give ourselves too much time. The danger is that we will become so attached to the leverage our wound gives us over the one who hurt us that we will never let it go. There's a lot of power in withheld forgiveness—the power of the leverage by which the wounded one controls the guilty one.

---

[1] Source unknown, but not original with me.

Ah, forgiveness. It's easy for those of us who don't have much to forgive. But some of us have more to forgive than others. And, for those who have the most to forgive, forgiveness can be a long journey. Sometimes the journey lasts so long that what began as anger finally turns to something more like sadness. And, sometimes, the journey doesn't get completed in this life, which is why so many of us talk to graves and hope for a heaven that includes conversations. So it's complicated, this journey of forgiveness, but it's a journey that we can, at least, begin. A good place to start might be simply to say, "*My spirit has been wounded. The person who hurt me is, like me, a flawed, complicated, wounded human being who is neither all bad nor all good, and both of us stand under the judgment of God and the mercy of God.* Starting there will not make forgiveness simple, easy, or automatic, but it will at least make it possible—which isn't much, I know, but you have to start somewhere, otherwise you end up like the person in the parable who, sadly, could not give, or receive, forgiveness.

Amen.

FOR THOSE WHO SIT IN DARKNESS

[68]"Blessed be the Lord God of Israel, for he has looked favourably on his people and redeemed them. [69]He has raised up a mighty saviour for us in the house of his servant David, [70]as he spoke through the mouth of his holy prophets from of old, [71]we would be saved from our enemies and from the hand of all who hate us. [72]Thus he has shown the mercy promised to our ancestors, and has remembered his holy covenant, [73]the oath that he swore to our ancestor Abraham, to grant us [74]that we, being rescued from the hands of our enemies, might serve him without fear, [75]in holiness and righteousness before him all our days. [76]And you, child, will be called the prophet of the Most High; for you will go before the Lord to prepare his ways, [77]to give knowledge of salvation to his people by the forgiveness of their sins. [78]By the tender mercy of our God, the dawn from on high will break upon us, [79]to give light to those who sit in darkness and in the shadow of death, to guide our feet into the way of peace." Luke 1:68–79

Two or three years ago I was driving down I-55 one day when I heard, on National Public Radio, an interview with a Catholic priest who years earlier had been given permission by Mother Teresa to compile and publish her letters and journals once she was gone. As he spoke about Mother Teresa's lifelong battle with a gnawing sense of distance from God, the priest said that, in one of her journals, Mother Teresa had written these words: *If I ever get to speak to Jesus, I think I'll just say, "All my life, I loved you in the darkness."*

One imagines that, in that regard, Mother Teresa was not alone. There is so much pain in this world; so much disappointment, guilt, remorse and anger, so many hidden burdens and secret shadows casting so much deep darkness across so many dear and good souls, that there must be many, who, given a chance to speak with Jesus, might well say the same: "*All my life, I loved you in the darkness.*"

The good news is that, apparently, *in the darkness* is also where Jesus loves us. According to Luke 1:79, that's where Jesus went when Jesus came, drawn to the darkness like a moth to a flame: "*By the tender mercy of our God, the dawn from on high will break upon us, to give light to those who sit in darkness.*" Wherever the deepest darkness is, that's where Jesus goes first, stays last, and does most.

This might be why the closer we get to Jesus, the more we are drawn to whomever is sitting in the deepest darkness. If you've ever wondered why you feel so drawn to those who bear the most crippling burdens and live in the most unbearable circumstances, if you've ever wondered what it is that always draws you to the loneliest soul in the nursing home or the poorest stranger on the street or the most marginalized person in the room, there's your answer: *It's the spirit of Jesus, drawing you into someone else's darkness.* After all, you can't walk with Jesus and not go where Jesus went, and that's where Jesus went when Jesus came: straight to the darkness, like a moth to a flame.[1]

The amazing thing about all that is this: *When we carry the light of God's love into someone else's darkness, our own darkness becomes lit by the light we carry to them.* It's amazing. You go where need is great or grief is deep, carrying the light of God's love in a meal or a check or a prayer or a visit or a plant or a cake, and your own darkness becomes lit by the light you

---

[1] "Like a moth to a flame" is of unknown origin.

carried into someone else's shadows. The light you shine into someone else's darkness spills back into your own, and by the time you get back home you aren't sure if you gave light or got light. You can't quite tell if you gave light to someone else for their darkness, or were given light for your own. You're just walking in the light now, and, when you're walking in the light, it's impossible to tell whether you're the shiner or the shinee.

Amen.

They Got That, We Get This

²¹Jesus had crossed again in the boat to the other side, a great crowd gathered round him; and he was by the lake. ²²Then one of the leaders of the synagogue named Jairus came and, when he saw him, fell at his feet ²³and begged him repeatedly, "My little daughter is at the point of death. Come and lay your hands on her, so that she may be made well, and live." ²⁴So he went with him. And a large crowd followed him and pressed in on him. ²⁵Now there was a woman who had been suffering from hemorrhages for twelve years. ²⁶She had endured much under many physicians, and had spent all that she had; and she was no better, but rather grew worse. ²⁷She had heard about Jesus, and came up behind him in the crowd and touched his cloak, ²⁸for she said, "If I but touch his clothes, I will be made well." ²⁹Immediately her hemorrhage stopped; and she felt in her body that she was healed of her disease. ³⁰Immediately aware that power had gone forth from him, Jesus turned about in the crowd and said, "Who touched my clothes?" ³¹And his disciples said to him, "You see the crowd pressing in on you; how can you say, 'Who touched me?'" ³²He looked all round to see who had done it. ³³But the woman, knowing what had happened to her, came in fear and trembling, fell down before him, and told him the whole truth. ³⁴He said to her, "Daughter, your faith has made you well; go in peace, and be healed of your disease." ³⁵While he was still speaking, some people came from the leader's house to say, "Your daughter is dead. Why trouble the teacher any further?" ³⁶But overhearing what they said, Jesus said to the leader of the synagogue, "Do not fear, only believe." ³⁷He allowed no one to follow him except Peter, James, and John, the brother of James. ³⁸When they came to the house of the leader of the synagogue,

he saw a commotion, people weeping and wailing loudly. [39]When he had entered, he said to them, "Why do you make a commotion and weep? The child is not dead but sleeping." [40]And they laughed at him. Then he put them all outside, and took the child's father and mother and those who were with him, and went in where the child was. [41]He took her by the hand and said to her, "Talitha cum," which means, "Little girl, get up!" [42]And immediately the girl got up and began to walk about (she was twelve years of age). At this they were overcome with amazement. [43]He strictly ordered them that no one should know this, and told them to give her something to eat. —Mark 5:21–43

I don't know about you, but I think I can say with certainty that I have never known anyone who got what Jairus got. I've known a lot of prayerful, faithful people, but I've never known anyone who lost a loved one to death and then had that loved one given back to them, alive and well. That's what Jairus and his family got. They got their loss reversed and their grief removed, just like that. That's what happened in Mark chapter 5.

This, of course, places some rather significant distance between what Jairus got and what we get. What Jairus and his family got was an instantaneous and perfect resolution for their misery, which is a beautiful and wonderful thing, but which is quite unlike what most of us experience most of the time. When we read Mark chapter 5, we are glad for Jairus and his daughter, as well as for the woman with the hemorrhage whom Jesus healed on his way to Jairus' house, but we also know that the way things worked out for them on the page is different from the way things usually work out for us on the ground. (I know that popular Christianity tells us that if we only had stronger faith, we would see such wonders all the time, that more faith from us would produce more miracles from God. But let's think about that for a moment. If that were true, that would mean that God is sitting up there unable, or unwilling, to act on our behalf unless and until we work up enough faith to persuade God to do the good thing God already knows we need. Is that really the way God is? I don't think so. I don't think God is holding out on our broken hearts and fragile lives, waiting to see if we can try a little harder to believe a little better. The idea that God is stuck in neutral, unable or unwilling to act on our behalf unless we give God the right amount of faith, is another expression of "transactional theology," the popular theology that sees our life with God as a series of "transactions": "*If I give God enough faith God will come around and do my will.*" God is better than that, and our theology should be better than that. The truth is, we don't know why we don't always get, down here on the ground, what Jairus got, back there on the page.)

When it comes to life's great struggles and griefs, instantaneously perfect resolutions are a lot less common down here on the ground than they are back there on the page. We get to see that kind of miracle sometimes, praise God. But, mostly, that seems to be what the people on the page got. As for us, we usually get something else.

Jairus and the woman with the hemorrhage got the sudden, perfect, total, complete, and instant transformation of their sorrow and grief, and *we get this*: We get a sanctuary full of people from whom we draw indescribable strength and inexplicable joy in the face of unbearable sorrow and fear. We get sixteen names on a caregiving card on Tuesday telling us sixteen people sat in a circle and prayed for us on Monday. We get food at the door or flowers on the porch or faces at the funeral or calls on the phone or notes in the mail. Jairus and the woman with the hemorrhage got sudden, total, complete, instantaneous relief, reversal, and resolution. *They got that, and we get this*: The sustaining, loving, praying, writing, calling family of faith; the song-singing, courage-raising, hope-lifting, hand-holding, strength-giving, casserole-delivering, burden-bearing, grief-sharing church of Jesus Christ.

Sometimes, of course, it happens for us on the ground as it happened for them on the page. Sometimes we do get what they got; the amazing, stunning, instantaneously perfect resolution to our struggle and grief. Needless to say, it's wonderful when it works out that way. And, sometimes it does, praise God. But, of course, the problem is, you never know. You never know whether or not you'll get something miraculous like the sick woman and the sad man got in Mark chapter 5. You never know about that.

What we do know is that even if we never get *that*, we'll always have *this*.

Amen.

If This Is a Crutch, I'll Take Two

²²Immediately he made the disciples get into the boat and go on ahead to the other side, while he dismissed the crowds. ²³And after he had dismissed the crowds, he went up the mountain by himself to pray. When evening came, he was there alone, ²⁴but by this time the boat, battered by the waves, was far from the land, for the wind was against them. ²⁵And early in the morning he came walking towards them on the lake. ²⁶But when the disciples saw him walking on the lake, they were terrified, saying, "It is a ghost!" And they cried out in fear. ²⁷But immediately Jesus spoke to them and said, "Take heart, it is I; do not be afraid." ²⁸Peter answered him, "Lord, if it is you, command me to come to you on the water." ²⁹He said, "Come." So Peter got out of the boat, started walking on the water, and came towards Jesus. ³⁰But when he noticed the strong wind, he became frightened, and beginning to sink, he cried out, "Lord, save me!" ³¹Jesus immediately reached out his hand and caught him, saying to him, "You of little faith, why did you doubt?" ³²When they got into the boat, the wind ceased. ³³And those in the boat worshipped him, saying, "Truly you are the Son of God." —Matthew 14:22–33

Across a lifetime of churchgoing I have heard, and preached, quite a few sermons based on this familiar gospel lesson, most of which went something like this: *If Peter had had more faith he would have done a better job of walking on water.* Then, a few years ago, I stumbled across a sermon by Barbara Brown Taylor that caused me to see this story in a different light. Reverend Taylor said that the real point of this passage was that if Peter had had more faith, he might have done a better job, not of walking on the water but of staying in the boat.[1] She based that way of reading this lesson on the fact that when Jesus identified himself to the disciples in the storm, only Peter raised a question and required a sign. In verse 27, when Jesus said, *"Take heart, it is I. Do not be afraid,"* only Peter responded, *"If it is you, command me to come to you on the water."* Only Peter said, *"If it is you."* The other disciples apparently had enough faith to take Jesus at his word, stay in the boat, and keep rowing until Jesus could get to them.

Thinking about the story that way sort of changes the way you read verse 31, where Jesus says to Peter, *"You of little faith, why did you doubt?"* I've always assumed that when Jesus said that, he was saying, *"Peter, if you'd had more faith you could have kept walking on the water."* It never occurred to me that he might have been saying, *"Peter, if you'd had more faith you would have been content to stay in the boat with the others, where you belonged."* That way of reading this passage turns the spotlight away from Peter's brief stroll and big splash and puts the focus on a more important lesson for the church and about the church, which is that Jesus' followers belong together, with one another, *in the boat*. You can actually watch that idea take shape by following the boat through the lesson: In verse 22, Jesus commands his disciples to get into the boat. In verse 29, Peter steps out of the boat, and quicker than you can say, *"Throw me an inner tube,"* he's in over his head. Then look at what verses 32 and 33 say: *When they got into the boat, the wind ceased. And those in the boat worshiped, saying, "Truly you are the Son of God."* Once everyone was back in the boat things were better. They were back where they belonged. They belonged in the boat, with one another.

---

[1] Barbara Brown Taylor, *Bread of Angels* (Boston: Cowley Publications, 1997) 121.

Charles E. Poole

And so do we. The longer I live, the more I know that ours is a one-another faith. In the Bible, life with God is life in community, *in the boat*, with one another. You have, no doubt, noticed the Bible's long list of "one anothers": *Love one another.... Forgive one another.... Bear with one another.... Pray for one another.... Confess your sins to one another.... Wait for one another.... Honor one another.... Speak the truth to one another.* That long list of "one anothers" reminds us that we belong in a community of faith, with one another, in the church.

That is not to suggest that the church is perfect. Far from it. The same church that can fill your heart can also break your heart. There is no perfect church, and to always be looking for one is to sentence ourselves to a life of perpetual discontentment. But, as flawed and limited as the church is, there are also wonders of grace that happen in church that don't happen anywhere else. It is in the church that our lives are formed for God. It is in the church that hard hearts are slowly softened for God and eventually opened to others. In the church our sins are declared forgiven. In the church we are compelled to care and sent to serve. In the church we get to sit in the same room every week with people who make us want to be better than we know how to be all by ourselves. It happens here. In the church. In the boat, together where we belong.

Every time any congregation of any faith gathers in any sanctuary, there is a lot of pain in the room. For many of us, life is not so easy. We get up every morning to face the same fears and fear the same faces, to battle the same demons, fight the same battles, and long for the same relief we longed for yesterday. No one is so strong or so special that they can bear such burdens alone. You get out there by yourself and you end up like Peter: drowning. We need one another. We belong in the boat.

A few years ago, *Baptists Today* conducted an interview with church historian Walter B. Shurden. In the course of the article, Dr. Shurden's thoughts turned to the church and his love for it and devotion to it, at which point he quoted his wife Kay as having once said, "*Buddy, if we woke up Sunday morning and discovered that the atheists were right, we'd still get dressed and go to church, because we need those people that much.*" It's true. We do. We do need to be surrounded by the people of God that much. We need one another. We belong in the boat.

William Sloane Coffin, former chaplain at Yale and pastor of Riverside Church in New York City, once heard someone dismiss such talk as this with the scornful assessment, "*The church is just a crutch,*" to which Dr. Coffin replied, "*Yes. Right. The church is a crutch. And what makes you think you aren't limping?*"

Amen.

A Church for Rachel

¹³Now after they had left, an angel of the Lord appeared to Joseph in a dream and said, "Get up, take the child and his mother, and flee to Egypt, and remain there until I tell you; for Herod is about to search for the child, to destroy him." ¹⁴Then Joseph got up, took the child and his mother by night, and went to Egypt, ¹⁵and remained there until the death of Herod. This was to fulfill what had been spoken by the Lord through the prophet, "Out of Egypt I have called my son." ¹⁶When Herod saw that he had been tricked by the wise men, he was infuriated, and he sent and killed all the children in and around Bethlehem who were two years old or under, according to the time that he had learned from the wise men. ¹⁷Then was fulfilled what had been spoken through the prophet Jeremiah: ¹⁸"A voice was heard in Ramah, wailing and loud lamentation, Rachel weeping for her children; she refused to be consoled, because they are no more." ¹⁹When Herod died, an angel of the Lord suddenly appeared in a dream to Joseph in Egypt and said, ²⁰"Get up, take the child and his mother, and go to the land of Israel, for those who were seeking the child's life are dead." ²¹Then Joseph got up, took the child and his mother, and went to the land of Israel. ²²But when he heard that Archelaus was ruling over Judea in place of his father Herod, he was afraid to go there. And after being warned in a dream, he went away to the district of Galilee. ²³There he made his home in a town called Nazareth, so that what had been spoken through the prophets might be fulfilled, "He will be called a Nazorean." —Matthew 2:13–23

One thing you can say about Lex; he doesn't leave the lights up long. I'm talking about our old Sunday morning Bible passage picking friend, Lex Shunnairy. Here we are, not even a week away from Christmas Day, and already the lectionary has led us far from the bright light of angels and stars, deep into the dark night of sorrow and loss.

I guess we should be used to that by now. After all, it does happen that way every three years. Every third year, on the first Sunday of Christmastide, the Common Lectionary requires us to stagger across the rugged terrain of this dimly-lit corner of Matthew, where, early on, we stumble over a question mark, which goes something like this: *"Would God really do that? Would God, who sees all human life as sacred, really warn one family to flee with their baby, but not warn the other families to flee with theirs?"* Careful speech requires us to give a voice to questions such as those because, if we're thinking while we're reading, we know they're in there somewhere.

If you're looking for the answers to those kinds of questions, well, sorry, you'll just have to keep looking. The fact is, there are some questions that can be answered, and there are other questions that must be allowed to stand, just as there are some tears that can be dried and other tears that can only be allowed to fall, a small river of which runs through the second chapter of Matthew: *"A voice was heard in Ramah, wailing and loud lamentation, Rachel weeping for her children; she refused to be consoled, because they are no more."* Here Matthew is quoting Jeremiah 31:15, where Jeremiah says that Rachel is weeping inconsolably for her children, who are no more. Jeremiah was writing many generations after the real Rachel had died giving birth to Benjamin, but when he needed an image to describe the awful sadness of the people of God being carried away captive into exile, Jeremiah reached back to the book of Genesis and brought Rachel forward as an image of unconsolable grief in the face of unbearable pain. Then, six centuries later, when Matthew needed an image to describe the unspeakable sorrow of Herod's massacre of toddlers and babies, Matthew also reached for Rachel as an image of unconsolable grief in the face of unbearable pain: "*Then was fulfilled what was spoken by the prophet Jeremiah,*" says Matthew in verse 17, "*A voice was heard in Ramah, wailing and loud lamentation, Rachel weeping for her children. She refused to be consoled, because they are no more.*" Once again Rachel's name is invoked to describe sorrow too deep for words; the sorrows no one expects to face; tragedies and struggles that are too much to bear, but must be borne, nonetheless; tragedies and struggles that leave us, like Rachel, unconsolable.

Matthew's words about Rachel's unconsolable grief in the face of unbearable loss call to mind a passage from Stanley Hauerwas' book *God, Medicine, and Suffering,* in which he says that what we need is not an explanation for our suffering, but rather "*A community capable of absorbing our grief.*"[1] For the Rachels of this world, for those who are living with unbearable pain and unconsolable grief, that may be the best we can be: "*A community capable of absorbing one another's grief.*" *Absorbing* one another's grief is, needless to say, quite a different matter than *explaining* one another's grief. Once upon a time, twenty or so years ago, I thought it was my job to explain the unbearable. I was a walking, talking Exhibit A for that line in Wendell Berry's novel *A Place on Earth* where Jayber Crow says, "*The worst thing about preachers is they think they've got to say*

---

[1] Stanley Hauerwas, *God, Medicine and Suffering* (Grand Rapids: Eerdmans, 1990) xi.

something whether anything can be said or not."[2] In the face of Rachel's tears, in the face of unconsolable grief, I would say things like, "*God won't put more on us than we can bear,*" or "*God makes no mistakes,*" or "*God didn't send this, God just allowed it.*" I was sincere and earnest in saying those things, but I guess it's now been twenty-something years since I've said those phrases or others like them. I finally realized that no one knows enough to be talking that way to the Rachels of this world about the God of this world. Careful speech requires us to say that we are not capable of explaining one another's losses. We are, however, capable of absorbing one another's grief, even the unconsolable grief that comes with unbearable pain.

Few people have spoken of all this more clearly and carefully than William Sloane Coffin. In a sermon he offered following the sudden and tragic loss of his son, Coffin spoke about those who came to console his family, saying, "*In my intense grief, I felt that some of my friends were quoting comforting words of scripture to me for their self-protection, to pretty up a situation the bleakness of which they simply couldn't face. But immediately after such a tragedy,* Coffin continued, *what you need is people who only want to hold your hand, not to quote anybody or say anything, people who simply bring food and flowers, people who sign letters, simply, "Your broken-hearted friend."*[3] Or, as Hauerwas said, "*What we need is a community capable of absorbing our grief.*"

We can be that, because we can do that. We cannot supply answers, but we can give support. We cannot explain suffering, but we can spread it and share it and somehow help absorb it.

---

[2] Wendell Berry, *A Place on Earth* (Washington DC: Counterpoint, 1999) 105.

[3] *A Cloud of Witnesses*, ed. Thomas G. Long and Cornelius Plating (Grand Rapids: Eerdmans, 1994) 264.

That is a high calling, and a deep one; and it is also a calling that requires us to live lives of quiet prayer and authentic holiness so we will be ready when we are needed. We have to practice being prayerful and thoughtful and gentle and kind on all the normal and routine days, so that, on the rare day of unbearable loss, we will be ready and able to help absorb the grief we cannot console.

To show up quietly with a flower or a casserole or a check or a pie, to remember to call or write or stay in touch, to walk with a devastated soul at the edge of a shadow the central darkness of which only they can fully know, is a fine and beautiful way for a person to live and a church to be. The Rachels of this world will always need a community capable of absorbing their grief, and we should always be ready to be that kind of community: a church for Rachel.

Amen.